TWO-WORD VERBS IN ENGLISH

TWO-WORD VERBS IN ENGLISH

J. N. Hook

HEINLE & HEINLE

THOMSON LEARNING

Australia Canada Mexico Singapore Spain United Kingdom United States

HEINLE & HEINLE

THOMSON LEARNING

Two-Word Verbs in English
J.N. Hook

For permission to use material from this text or product contact us:
Tel: 1-800-730-2214
Fax: 1-800-730-2215
Web: www.thomsonrights.com

ISBN: 0-15-592506-7

Library of Congress Catalog Card Number:
    80-83748

PREFACE

Teachers of English as a second language have long realized the need for supplementary materials, especially on idiomatic English. The aim of this book is to fill that need.

Two-Word Verbs in English instructs students in an aspect of English that is especially difficult for learners of English as a second language. The book is for intermediate and advanced students—those with moderate reading skills and a grasp of basic English grammar. It aims to help them to speak and write in English in an idiomatic and natural way. Two- and three-word verbs are an indispensable tool to speaking English naturally.

These verbs are sometimes also called phrasal verbs, merged verbs, and verb-adverb or verb-preposition combinations. Between three and four thousand such verbs exist in modern English, and more continue to be added to the language. Some of these verbs are among the most commonly used verbs in English. Students may have difficulty learning them because, although each part of a two- or three-word verb is simple and ordinary, their combination often turns out to have an unpredictable and unexpected meaning.

Consider the verb *turn out*, in the preceding sentence. The student may know the meaning of *turn*, but here nothing seems to be "turning." Neither is anything going "out" in the usual sense. Students need help in learning that the meaning is "to result" or "to be found to be." For another example, consider the three-word verb *put up with*, as in "Both teachers and students must *put up with* many problems." In that sentence, nothing seems to be "put" or "up" or "with." English speakers must learn to attach the meaning "tolerate" to that unlikely combination of words.

Two-Word Verbs in English attempts to help students to *understand* and *use* many of the most common two- and three-word verbs in English. At the same time, it gives them *practice in other phases of English*. Here are the book's special features:

1. While teaching over 400 widely used two- and three-word verbs, it simultaneously provides practice in such other skills as silent and oral reading, forming questions and answers, using irregular verbs (*break, write*, etc.), using present and past participles (*going, gone*, etc.), forming imperative sentences, using negatives, and using the passive voice.

2. At the beginning of each of the fifteen chapters, a short narrative provides a focus for most of the exercises that follow. These 300- to 500-word narratives all concern members of one

family, the Jacksons: George and Edna Jackson; their college son, Tom; and the twins in high school, Jane and Jim. The readings thus offer more human interest than would unrelated sentence drills. The reader observes, for instance, college and school activities of the young people and also observes the members of the family as they get up in the morning, go about their work, talk about their financial problems, set out on a short trip, and attempt to start a small business. These stories show how to use many of the two-word verbs that are common in school, the home, travel, physical activity, and business. About twenty-five to thirty such verbs are used in each narrative.

3. Following the narrative, a glossary defines and again illustrates the newly introduced two-word verbs, giving the principal parts of each. It also indicates whether each verb is intransitive (like *sit down*), separable (like *find . . . out . . .*), or nonseparable (like *wait on* _____). These distinctions are important for accurate use, and such simple graphic devices as ellipses and blank lines help the student to remember them.

4. The exercises in each chapter begin with silent and oral reading of the narrative and end with the construction of original sentences using the two- and three-word verbs introduced in the chapter. In between, the varied exercises include substituting two-word verbs for their synonyms, forming questions, using different tense forms, and pantomiming. In all, some twenty different sorts of exercises are included, but they always culminate in the requirement that students *use* the verbs in sentences that they themselves must construct.

5. Following the fifteen chapters, a cumulative review section provides a review of all the verbs that have been covered in the earlier chapters. Through doing these exercises, students can test themselves on their retention and use of the verbs that have been presented earlier.

The aim of the book is to teach students to *use* these verbs, not only in this book, but in their daily interactions with people at school and at work. The student who has mastered the verbs treated here should have little difficulty using the two- and three-word verbs that he or she is certain to run into when reading or speaking English anywhere.

J. N. HOOK

CONTENTS

Cumulative Review

Answer Key   173

Verb Index   196

Introduction

WHAT TWO-WORD VERBS ARE

TWO-WORD VERB	MEANING	EXAMPLES
give up	stop trying, surrender	Ali and Dave are working on a problem, but Dave *gives up*.
stand for	represent, mean	In the problem, D *stands for* the diameter of the circle.
pick up	lift, gather into one's hands or arms	Dave *picks* his books *up* and goes to class.

Give up, stand for, and *pick up* are examples of two-word verbs. English has many such verbs.

The two words together often have the same meaning as a one-word verb. Each of the two words often does not have its usual meaning, however. For example, in *give up,* nobody "gives" and nothing goes "up."

A few verbs that you will study have three words rather than two:

catch up with	come to (someone) from behind, overtake	Sam *catches up with* Roy.
brush up on	study again, review	Tom is *brushing up on* his science.

Two-word verbs are not the same as a simple verb with a preposition.

Simple Verb and a Preposition

SUBJECT	SIMPLE VERB	PREPOSITION	OBJECT OF PREPOSITION
Jane	ran	across	the grass.

Two-Word Verb

SUBJECT	TWO-WORD VERB	OBJECT OF VERB
Jane	ran across	an old friend.

In the first sentence Jane really *ran*. She really moved *across* the grass. But in the second sentence she did not *run*, and she did not move *across* her friend. *Ran across* in the second sentence means "met" or "happened to see." The two words act together as a single verb would act.

KINDS OF TWO-WORD VERBS

NAME OF VERB   EXAMPLES

I (Intransitive)	**give up**	The baby tried to walk but then *gave up*.
Has no object of the verb.	**get along**	''We'll *get along* well,'' Tom said.
NS (Nonseparable)		
Has an object at the end.	**go after** ___	Pedro *goes after* a BOOK.
May not be separated by an object.	**look for** ___	Helen *looked for* an ARTICLE.
	catch up with ___	Dave *caught up with* LEE.
S (Separable)	**hand** . . . **in** . . .	Tom *handed in* the PAPER.
Has an object at the end or between the parts.		Tom *handed* the PAPER *in*.
		Tom *handed* IT *in*.
	tear . . . **up** . . .	Helen *tears up* some old SHIRTS.
		Helen *tears* some old SHIRTS *up*.
		Helen *tears* THEM *up*.

Note 1: When a pronoun like *it* or *them* is the object of a separable verb, it always goes between the parts:

> Tom *handed* IT *in*. (Not: Tom *handed in* IT.)
> Helen *tears* THEM *up*.

Note 2: A few separable verbs have objects in both places:

> Maria *tried* her PLAN *out* on DAVE. (*Plan* and *Dave* are the objects.)
> (or) Maria *tried out* her PLAN *on* DAVE.

HOW TO USE THIS BOOK TO LEARN TWO-WORD VERBS

Each chapter starts with a little story that uses twenty to thirty two-word verbs. Then a glossary tells you what these verbs mean.

Read the story several times. Read it aloud if possible. While you read, try to guess the meaning of each verb in italic type, like this: ***heading for***. Use the glossary to find whether you were right.

In each story and in the glossary, one part of each two- or three-word verb is in different type, called boldface italic: ***hand . . . in . . . .*** Pronounce that part a little more strongly. (See page 12 for more information on pronunciation.)

Several exercises follow each glossary. These exercises will help you to learn and remember the verbs.

The last exercise in each chapter asks you to write or say several original sentences. These will show that you really understand and can use the two- or three-word verbs.

PRONUNCIATION OF PEOPLE'S NAMES

The pronunciations given here are those usually heard in the United States. Stressed syllables are in boldface italic type.

ā as in d*ay*   o͞o as in m*oo*n
ă as in r*a*n   û as in f*ur* or h*er*
ä as in f*a*ther or h*o*t   ə as in *a*cross or sof*a*
ē as in s*ee*   ch as in *ch*ild
ĕ as in r*e*d   th as in *th*in
ĭ as in h*i*ll   ~~th~~ as in *th*ey
ō as in g*o*   oi as in b*oy*
ô as in *o*rder

Names of Principal Characters

Dave   *dāv*
Edna   *ĕd* nə
George   *jôrj*
Helen   *hĕl* ən
Jane   *jān*

Jim   *jĭm*
Lee (often a Chinese name)   *lē*
Maria (often Spanish)   ma *rē* ə
Pedro (often Spanish)   *pā* drō
Tom   *tŏm*

Other Names Mentioned

Ahmed (usually Arabic)   *ä* mĕd
Ali (usually Arabic)   ä *lē*
Andy   *ăn* dē
Betty   *bĕt* ē
Bill   *bĭl*
Billy   *bĭl* ē
Brendan (often Irish)   *brĕn* dən
Cynthia   *sĭn* thē ə
Don   *dŏn*
Ella   *ĕl* ə
Fernando (often Spanish)   fûr *năn* dō
Fred   *frĕd*
Hedda (usually German or Scandinavian)   *hĕd* ə

Henry   *hĕn* rē
Jack   *jăk*
Joanna   jō *ăn* ə
Nina   *nē* nə
Rachel (often Jewish)   *rā* chəl
Roy   *roi*
Sally   *săl* ē
Sam   *săm*
Sigrid (usually Scandinavian)   *sĭg* rəd
Suki (usually Japanese)   *so͞o* kē
Susan   *so͞o* zən
Wanda   *wän* də
Yuki (usually Japanese)   yo͞o kē

1. School Life

Getting Along in One's Schoolwork

Tom Jackson and Dave Page were *heading for* the library. Lee Choy and Pedro Garcia *caught up with* them.

"Are you *going after* a book?" Lee asked Tom.

"Yes," said Tom. "I need to *look for* another book about airplanes. I was *checking* my paper *over*, and I *found out* that I had *put in* some wrong information."

"I have to *look up* an article," Dave added. "My history teacher asked us to *read through* a long article. *Keeping up with* that course is difficult for me. I'm always *falling behind*. That's because I *put off* doing my assignments."

"So do I," said Pedro. "Right now I'm writing a paper for my science class. I *tore* the first paper *up* because it was bad. Now I have several new ideas, and I've been *trying* them *out on* my friend Maria. I have to *hand* the paper *in* on Monday. I also need to *brush up on* my mathematics, but I can't *figure out* the meanings of some of those strange-looking signs."

"I know what you mean," Dave told him. "I don't know what some of the signs *stand for*, either."

"I need to *make up* a test," Tom said. "I missed it when I was sick. But I'll wait until I have *turned in* my paper on airplanes. I keep a list of things I should do, and I *cross* them *off* one by one as I do them."

"You're so systematic, Tom," Dave said, smiling. "You always plan everything. I should *put together* a list, too, but it would be too long. I would just *give up*."

"I sometimes want to *give up*, too," said Tom, "but then I think that I'll *pull through* somehow. Studying so much is hard, but usually we *get along* rather well. We just have to *keep at* it."

"Yes," Lee said, "we do. But sometimes I'd like to *get away* from it all."

GLOSSARY

Notes: When a blank follows a verb in this glossary, it means that an object is used in that place: **get** *away* **from** ____ .

When there are two short dotted lines with the verb, an object is used in one place or the other: **hand** . . . *in* . . . .

The definitions given here are those you need for the story you are reading in this chapter. The same verb may also have other, somewhat different meanings. Sometimes other definitions will be given later. In some glossaries you will notice "See ____" or "See also ____ ." "See ____" gives the chapter where the verb was defined earlier. "See also ____" shows that a different definition has been given earlier.

The abbreviations I, NS, and S have been explained on page 3.

INFINITIVE	PAST TENSE	PAST PARTICIPLE	
brush *up* **on** ____	**brushed up on**	**[have] brushed up on**	(NS)

study again, review, refresh one's memory about
> Tom is *brushing up on* his chemistry.

catch *up* **with** ____	**caught up with**	**[have] caught up with**	(NS)

come to someone from behind, overtake
> Pedro *caught up with* Maria.

check . . . *over* . . .	**checked over**	**[have] checked over**	(S)

take another look at, try to find mistakes in, examine
> One should *check over* an examination paper.

cross . . . *off* . . .	**crossed off**	**[have] crossed off**	(S)

mark out, cancel (*Cross out* is often used for the same meaning.)
> Some people *cross off* each day on a calendar.

fall be*hind*	**fell behind**	**[have] fallen behind**	(I)

fail to do work, etc., by a certain time; move more slowly than (someone else)
> Dave *fell behind* in his history class. In a race, Tom *fell behind*.

(Also may be NS, with an object after *behind*: He *fell behind* the other students.)

figure . . . *out* . . .	**figured out**	**[have] figured out**	(S)

find (an answer or a solution), decide, learn, understand
> Helen *figured out* the answer.

find . . . *out* . . .	**found out**	**[have] found out**	(S)

discover, learn
> Helen's friend told her a lie, but Helen *found out* the truth.

get a*long*	**got along**	**[have] got** or **gotten along**	(I)

do (one's work, etc.) well enough, manage, succeed fairly well
> In schoolwork some students *get along* better than others.

get a*way*	**got away**	**[have] got** or **gotten away**	(I)

escape, leave (something dangerous or bad) (often followed by *from*)
> "*Get away* from me," Yuki said to the growling dog.
> "*Get away!*"

give *up*   **gave up**   **[have] given up**   (I)
    stop trying, surrender
        The problem was difficult, but Tom would not *give up*.
    (Also S, stop doing something: Helen's father *gave up* smoking. He *gave* it *up*.)

***go* after** _____   **went after**   **[have] gone after**   (NS)
    go to get (something)
        Ali *went after* some ice cream.

hand . . . ***in*** . . .   **handed in**   **[have] handed in**   (S)
    give to a teacher, etc., pass in, submit (= *turn in*)
        "You should *hand* your papers *in* on Friday," the teacher said.

***head* for** _____   **headed for**   **[have] headed for**   (NS)
    go toward
        Ahmed *headed for* his next class.

***keep* at** _____   **kept at**   **[have] kept at**   (NS)
    continue to try (especially something difficult or tiresome), persist in
        Dave could solve the problem if he *kept at* it.

keep *up* with _____   **kept up with**   **[have] kept up with**   (NS)
    stay even with, stay beside (in a race, etc.), do what is necessary for (the opposite of
    fall behind)
        Pedro *kept up with* Maria.

***look* for** _____   **looked for**   **[have] looked for**   (NS)
    try to find, seek
        Suki was *looking for* a present for her mother.

look . . . ***up*** . . .   **looked up**   **[have] looked up**   (S)
    search for and find (especially in printed matter)
        Helen *looked up* some facts about early American history.

make . . . ***up*** . . .   **made up**   **[have] made up**   (S)
    take or do (an examination, a paper, etc.) that one has missed
        If you miss a test, you must *make* it *up*.

pull *through*   **pulled through**   **[have] pulled through**   (I)
    succeed or recover after some difficulty, get well after an illness, survive,
    come to a good ending
        The final examinations were hard, but most students *pulled through*.
    (Also S: The doctor said, "I'll *pull* her *through*.")

put . . . ***in*** . . .   **put in**   **[have] put in**   (S)
    include, add
        Rachel likes to *put in* many details when she writes.

put . . . ***off*** . . .   **put off**   **[have] put off**   (S)
    delay doing, postpone, avoid doing
        Sigrid sometimes *puts off* studying.

put ... **together** ...   **put together**   **[have] put together**   (S)
   bring separate parts together, compile, assemble
      Dave *put* the pieces of a puzzle *together*.

read ... **through** ...   **read** (rĕd) **through**   **[have] read** (rĕd) **through**   (S)
   read all of, read completely
      Nina *read through* two chapters.

stand for   **stood for**   **[have] stood for**   (NS)
   mean, represent, symbolize
      "Let x *stand for* the father's age," the mathematics teacher said.

tear ... **up** ...   **tore up**   **[have] torn up**   (S)
   tear into pieces, destroy by tearing into pieces
      Dave *tore* some old papers *up*.

try ... **out on** ...   **tried out on**   **[have] tried out on**   (S)
   get (someone else's) opinion of (Requires two objects. One of the objects may
   be after *out*.)
      Maria *tried out* her idea *on* Pedro.
      Maria *tried* her idea *out on* Pedro.

turn ... **in** ...   **turned in**   **[have] turned in**   (S)
   give to a teacher, etc., pass in, submit. (= *hand in*)
      Two students *turned* their papers *in* late.

EXERCISES

1. Reading

Read "Getting Along in One's Schoolwork" several times. Each student may then read a paragraph aloud.

2. Using Past Tenses and Past Participles

This chapter's glossary shows the past tense and the past participle of each verb. Note that *have*, *has*, or *had* require the past participle.

The following sentences are in the present tense. Read each of them. Change the present tense to the past tense. Then, use *have* (plural or with the subject *you* or *I*) or *has* (singular) and the past participle. Read the new sentences aloud.

EXAMPLE: Rachel *brushes up on* her Spanish.

Rachel brushed up on her Spanish.

Rachel has brushed up on her Spanish.

1. Maria and Joanna *catch up with* Elena.

   _____

   _____

2. Tom *checks over* his paper.

   _____

   _____

3. Brendan *falls behind* in his history course.

   _____

   _____

4. Helen *finds out* the truth.

   _____

   _____

5. The cat *gets away from* the dog.

   _____

   _____

6. Dave *gives up* too easily.

   _____

   _____

7. The boys *go after* some sandwiches.

    _____

    _____

8. The girls *hand* their papers *in*.

    _____

    _____

9. Betty *keeps at* her studies until midnight.

    _____

    _____

10. Maria *makes up* two short lists.

    _____

    _____

11. I *put off* my English.

    _____

    _____

12. The letters in the problem *stand for* weight and height.

    _____

    _____

13. Ella *tears* the cloth *up*.

    _____

    _____

14. Helen and Maria *try out* their plan *on* the boys.

    _____

    _____

15. Pedro *turns* his assignment *in* early.

    _____

    _____

3. Substituting

In the following sentences synonyms have been used for two-word and three-word verbs. What two- or three-word verb could be used instead of the italicized part of each sentence? (The first word is given.) Read or say your whole sentence. Be sure to use the correct form (present or past tense or past participle) of the verb.

EXAMPLE: Tom was *trying to find mistakes in* his paper. (check) *Tom was checking over his paper.*

1. Tom and Dave were *going toward* the library. (head) _____
   _____

2. Lee and Pedro *came up to* them *from behind*. (catch) _____
   _____

3. "Are you *going to get* a book?" Lee asked Tom. (go) _____
   _____

4. Yes. I need to *try to find* a book about airplanes. (look) _____
   _____

5. I was *taking another look at* my paper. (check) _____
   _____

6. I *discovered* that some of my statements were wrong. (find) _____
   _____

7. I had *included* some wrong information. (put) _____
   _____

8. "I have to *search for and find* an article," said Dave. (look) _____
   _____

9. My history teacher asked me to *read all of* it. (read) _____
   _____

10. I have trouble in *doing what is necessary for* that course. (keep) _____
    _____

11. I'm always *failing to do the work on time*. (fall) _____
    _____

12. That's because I *delay* doing my assignments. (put) _____
    _____

13. Pedro said, "I *tore into pieces* a paper for my science class." (tear) ____
    _____

14. I've been *getting* Maria's *opinion of* some new ideas. (try) (Use Maria.) ____
    _____

4. Substituting

Continue as in Exercise 3.

1. Pedro added, "I must *give* the paper *to the teacher* on Monday." (hand) ____
   _____

2. I also need to *review* my mathematics. (brush) _____

_____

3. It is hard for me to *understand* the meanings of some of the signs. (figure) _____

_____

4. Dave told him, "I don't know what some of the signs *represent*, either." (stand) _____

_____

5. Tom said, "I need to *take* a test *that I missed*." (make) _____

_____

6. I'll wait until I have *given to the teacher* my paper on airplanes. (turn) _____

_____

7. I list the things that I need to do, and I *mark* them *out* one by one as I do them. (cross) _____

_____

8. "I should *assemble* a list, too," said Dave. (put) _____

_____

9. But it would be so long that I would just *stop trying*. (give) _____

_____

10. "I think that I'll *succeed* in chemistry *after some hard work*," said Tom. (pull) _____

_____

11. Somehow we *manage*. (get) _____

_____

12. We just have to *continue to try* it. (keep) _____

_____

13. "Yes," Lee said, "but sometimes I'd rather *escape* from it." (get) _____

_____

PRONUNCIATION OF TWO- AND THREE-WORD VERBS

Most speakers stress the words or syllables in the ways shown below in boldface italic type.

Intransitive and separable verbs: In verbs marked I and S in the glossary, pronounce the second word a little more strongly.

Henry *gave **up***.
Helen *handed **in*** the paper.
Helen *handed* the paper ***in***.
Helen and Maria *get **along*** well in their work.

Exception: With separable verbs, if the object names something not mentioned before, stress that object.

The teacher said, "Don't *put* your **lessons** *off*."

Nonseparable verbs: Pronounce the first word a little more strongly in verbs marked NS in the glossary.

Dave **looked** *for* another book.

Three-word verbs: Pronounce the second word most strongly.

Andy *caught* **up** *with* Sigrid.

5. Practicing Pronunciation

Read "Getting Along in One's Schoolwork" again, aloud if possible. Be especially careful about stressing (accenting) slightly the words or syllables in boldface italic type.

6. Using Separable Verbs

Read once more "Kinds of Two-Word Verbs," page 3.

Here are some parts of sentences with S verbs. Make three sentences with each. Show where each object may be placed.

EXAMPLE: Look up in the library.   (the article, it)

Look up the article in the library.

Look the article up in the library.

Look it up in the library.

1. Nina *checks over.*   (each paper, it)

_____

_____

_____

2. Hedda *tore up.*   (several pages, them)

_____

_____

_____

3. She *figured out.*   (them, the answers)

_____

_____

_____

4. Dave *looked up.*   (an old magazine, it)

_____

_____

_____

5. Tom *made up* on Tuesday.   (a test, it)

_____

_____

_____

6. He had *turned in* on Monday.   (it, his paper)

_____

_____

_____

7. He made a list of assignments and *crossed off* one by one.   (the items, them)

_____

_____

_____

8. Lee disliked studying, and he kept *putting off*.   (it, his history lesson)

_____

_____

_____

9. He *handed in* late.   (his paper, it)

_____

_____

_____

10. Tom *put together*.   (it, a list)

_____

_____

_____

7. Making Up Original Sentences

Use some of these verbs to explain what you did when you prepared an assignment for one of your classes.

go after ____	keep at ____	hand . . . in . . .
look . . . up . . .	put . . . in . . .	turn . . . in . . .
read . . . through . . .	tear . . . up . . .	put . . . together . . .
look for ____	try . . . out on . . .	
put . . . off . . .	check . . . over . . .	

_____

_____

_____

14

_____

_____

_____

_____

_____

Use some of these verbs to talk or write about your studies.

brush up on ____	find . . . out . . .	look . . . up . . .
cross . . . off . . .	get along	make . . . up . . .
fall behind	give up	pull through
figure . . . out . . .	keep up with ____	

_____

_____

_____

_____

_____

_____

_____

_____

_____

2. Home Life (I)

Getting Up with the Jacksons

The alarm clock in Mr. and Mrs. Jackson's bedroom *goes off* at 6:30 A.M. Sleepily, Mr. Jackson reaches toward it to *turn* it *off*. He *gives up* trying to reach it and lets it *run down*.

By now Mrs. Jackson is awake. She *turns on* the light beside the bed and shakes her husband. "It's time to *get up*, George," she tells him.

"Aw—don't—" he mutters. But she *keeps on* shaking him until he too is awake. He *sits up*, but his eyes are still closed. Finally he *stands up*.

Mrs. Jackson *puts on* a bathrobe. Mr. Jackson *goes in* to take a shower and, awake at last, goes downstairs to set the table. In the kitchen Mrs. Jackson *plugs in* the coffee maker. She wants to boil eggs but remembers that they *used up* the eggs yesterday. She puts bread into the toaster and waits for it to *pop up*. Mr. Jackson puts cereal, milk, and juice on the table.

Then Mrs. Jackson *lets out* the cat. She calls the sixteen-year-old twins. "Breakfast!" she shouts. "Jim! Jane!"

In a few minutes all four are at the table. "What in the world do you *have on*?" Jim asks Jane.

"I forgot to *wash out* my clothes last night, so this morning I *hunted up* these things to wear."

"I thought you had *given* those old things *away* long ago," Jim tells her. "They look shabby."

"Leave me alone!" she says angrily.

"Children," Mrs. Jackson begs, "please don't *get into* a fight. I'm *running out of* patience with both of you. I don't *feel like* listening to another argument. Tom did not often argue before he left for college. Jane, you should *put* your clothes *away*. Then you could find something better to wear. I've told both of you again and again, 'Please *hang up* your clothes.'"

George Jackson is reading the newspaper. He laughs softly. "If you *come across* something funny or even interesting, you might *let us in on* it," his wife says.

"I'm just *looking at* the sports pages, Edna," he tells her. "You usually don't *care for* professional sports."

She goes to *see about* the cat and *lets* it *in*. The twins *pick up* their schoolbooks and go to school. George *puts* his coat *on*. As he *sets out* for work, he says to his wife, "Have a good day, Edna."

GLOSSARY

INFINITIVE	PAST TENSE	PAST PARTICIPLE	
care **for** _____	**cared for**	[**have**] **cared for**	(NS)

enjoy, like (generally preceded by *not* or used in a question) (*Care about* _____ has the same meaning.)
> Many children do not *care for* cooked vegetables.
> Would you *care for* some vegetables?

come **across** _____	**came across**	[**have**] **come across**	(NS)

find, happen to find, notice, see
> Andy *came across* an old photograph.

feel **like** _____	**felt like**	[**have**] **felt like**	(NS)

want (to), desire, have a wish (for or to) (usually followed by an *-ing* word)
> Do you *feel like* going to a movie?

get **into** _____	**got into**	[**have**] **got** or **gotten into**	(NS)

enter, start (a fight), become engaged in
> The twins *got into* the car.
> Then they *got into* an argument.

get *up*	**got up**	[**have**] **got** or **gotten up**	(I)

rise (from bed or any sitting or lying position)
> Many Americans *get up* very early.

give . . . *away* . . .	**gave away**	[**have**] **given away**	(S)

give, make a present of
> The twins *gave away* their clothes that were too small.

give . . . *up* . . .	**gave up**	[**have**] **given up**	(S)

stop (doing something), abandon, relinquish
> Fernando *gave up* smoking last year.

(Also I. See Chapter 1)

go *in*	**went in**	[**have**] **gone in**	(I)

enter, move from one place into another
> Edna opened the door and *went in*.

go *off*	**went off**	[**have**] **gone off**	(I)

ring, sound (an alarm clock or a similar device)
> My alarm clock did not *go off* this morning.

hang . . . *up* . . .	**hung up**	[**have**] **hung up**	(S)

place on a hanger or hook, etc.
> Mr. Jackson *hung* some tools *up* in his garage.

(Also I, end a telephone conversation: She finished talking on the phone and *hung up*.)

have . . . *on* . . .	**had on**	[**have**] **had on**	(S)

wear, be dressed in
> Edna still *had* her bathrobe *on*.

hunt . . . *up* . . .	**hunted up**	[**have**] **hunted up**	(S)

look for and find
> Jim *hunted up* his old baseball.

keep on _____	**kept on**	[have] **kept on**	(NS)

continue, persist in (usually followed by an -*ing* word)
> The clock *kept on* ringing.
> (Also I: Please *keep on*.)

let . . . *in* . . .	**let in**	[have] **let in**	(S)

allow to come in; open a door, etc., to admit
> Mrs. Jackson *let in* her neighbors' little boy.

let . . . *in* on . . .	**let in on**	[have] **let in on**	(S)

allow someone else to share (some information) (requires an object in each blank)
> Please tell us. *Let* us *in on* the secret.

let . . . *out* . . .	**let out**	[have] **let out**	(S)

allow to go out; open a door, etc., to permit an exit
> After a few minutes she *let* the little boy *out*.

look at _____	**looked at**	[have] **looked at**	(NS)

read, read quickly, examine, observe, pay attention to, watch
> Have you *looked at* prices of fresh fruit lately?

pick . . . *up* . . .	**picked up**	[have] **picked up**	(S)

lift, take into one's hands
> Please *pick up* those three little boxes.

plug . . . *in* . . .	**plugged in**	[have] **plugged in**	(S)

start (a toaster, etc.) by putting its plug into an electrical outlet
> The machine will not work unless you *plug* it *in*.

pop *up*	**popped up**	[have] **popped up**	(I)

rise suddenly
> A child's head *popped up* behind the chair.

put . . . *away* . . .	**put away**	[have] **put away**	(S)

put (something) where it should be or usually is
> Fred generally *puts* his tools *away*.

put . . . *on* . . .	**put on**	[have] **put on**	(S)

place a dress or other garment on oneself or someone else
> Jim *put on* his blue socks.
> The baby's mother *put* his shoes *on* for him.

run *down*	**ran down**	[have] **run down**	(I)

become unwound, stop going (a clock, an alarm, etc.)
> His clock *ran down* because he had not wound it.

run *out* of _____	**ran out of**	[have] **run out of**	(NS)

lose (patience), come to the end of (usually money or time)
> George wanted to buy and read several magazines, but he *ran out of* time and money.

see about _____	**saw about**	[have] **seen about**	(NS)

attend to, take care of, check the safety of
> Mothers and fathers often get up at night to *see about* the baby.

set *out*   **set out**   **[have] set out**   (I)
    start (a trip) (often followed by *on*)
        Mr. Jackson *sets out* for work five mornings each week.
        The sailors *set out* in January on their long journey.

sit *up*   **sat up**   **[have] sat up**   (I)
    change from a lying to a sitting position
        George was still sleepy, but finally he *sat up*.

stand *up*   **stood up**   **[have] stood up**   (I)
    change to a standing position
        Jim *stood up* too quickly and bumped his head against a tree branch.

turn . . . *off* . . .   **turned off**   **[have] turned off**   (S)
    stop (the water, light, clock, television, etc.)
        Don't forget to *turn off* the television.

turn . . . *on* . . .   **turned on**   **[have] turned on**   (S)
    start (the water, light, clock, television, etc.)
        Mr. Jackson *turned* the hot water *on*.

use . . . *up* . . .   **used up**   **[have] used up**   (S)
    use all of
        Jane has *used up* her paper.

wash . . . *out* . . .   **washed out**   **[have] washed out**   (S)
    wash, launder, wash lightly, rinse
        Some travelers *wash out* some of their clothes every night.

EXERCISES

1. Reading

Read "Getting Up with the Jacksons" several times. Each student may perhaps read a paragraph aloud.

2. Substituting

In the following sentences synonyms have been used for the two-word or three-word verbs. What would be the correct form of the two-word or three-word verb? (Remember that in the present tense a singular subject—except *I* and *you*—requires a final *s*: Jane turn*s* the light off.) Be ready to read your sentence aloud.

1. The alarm in the Jacksons' bedroom *rings* at 6:30. (go) _____

_____

2. Mr. Jackson reaches over to *stop* it. (turn) _____

_____

3. He *abandons* the effort. (give) _____

_____

4. He lets it *become unwound*. (run) _____

_____

5. Mrs. Jackson *starts* the light. (turn) _____

_____

6. "It's time to *rise from bed*," she tells her husband. (get) _____

_____

7. She *continues* shaking him. (keep) _____

_____

8. Finally he *changes to a sitting position*. (sit) _____

_____

9. Then he *changes to a standing position*. (stand) _____

_____

10. Mrs. Jackson *places* a bathrobe *on herself*. (put) _____

_____

11. Mr. Jackson *enters* to take a shower. (go) _____

_____

12. In the kitchen Mrs. Jackson *puts the plug of* the coffee maker *into an electrical outlet.* (plug)

_____

13. She remembers that she *used all of* the eggs yesterday. (use) _____

_____

14. She waits for the bread in the toaster to *rise suddenly.* (pop) _____

_____

15. She *opens the door to allow* the cat *to go out.* (let) _____

_____

3. Substituting

Continue as in Exercise 2.

1. Jim asks Jane, "What in the world *are* you *wearing*?" (have) (Hint: Use *do you* before the two-word verb.) _____

_____

2. "I forgot to *launder* my clothes last night," she tells him. (wash) _____

_____

3. So this morning I had to *look for and find* something else. (hunt) _____

_____

4. "I thought you had *made a present of* those old things long ago," Jim tells her. (give) _____

_____

5. "Children," says Mrs. Jackson, "please don't *start* a fight." (get) _____

_____

6. I'm *coming to the end of* patience. (run) _____

_____

7. I *don't want to* listen to another argument. (feel) (Hint: Use *listening* instead of *listen.*)

_____

8. Jane, if you would *put* your clothes *where they belong*, you could easily find something better to wear. (put) _____

_____

9. I've often told you, "Please *put* your clothes *on hangers.*" (hang) _____

_____

10. Mrs. Jackson says to her husband, "If you *happen to find* something interesting, you might tell us." (come) _____

_____

11. You should *share with* us whatever is funny. (let) _____

_____

12. I'm just *reading* the sports pages. (look) _____

_____

13. You don't *enjoy* professional sports. (care) _____

_____

14. Edna *attends to* the cat and *opens the door to allow* it *to come in*. (see, let) _____

_____

15. The twins *lift with their hands* their schoolbooks. (pick) _____

_____

16. George *starts* for the place where he works. (set) _____

_____

4. Using Past Tense Forms

In Exercises 2 and 3 the verbs you used are mainly in the present tense. Change the following to the past tense: sentences 3, 5, 7, 8, 9, 10, 11, 12, and 15 of Exercise 2; sentences 14, 15, and 16 of Exercise 3.

> EXAMPLE: The alarm in the Jacksons' bedroom *goes off*.
> Past: The alarm in the Jacksons' bedroom *went off*.

5. Using Past Participles

Change the same sentences as in Exercise 4. This time use *have* or *has* and the past participle.

> EXAMPLE: The alarm in the Jacksons' bedroom has *gone off*.

6. Making Up Pantomimes

When you do a pantomime, you pretend to perform an action. For example, to pantomime *turn off* you could reach for an imaginary alarm clock and make the motion of turning it off.

A pantomime may be done in front of the whole class or in small groups. The teacher may change some of the instructions.

For the following pantomime four students may work together. Follow this example, but make any necessary changes:

Student 1: Please turn off the alarm clock.
Student 2: (Does the pantomime. He or she pretends to turn off an alarm clock.)
Student 3: Did (he, she) turn off the alarm clock?
Student 4: Yes, (he, she) turned it off like this. (Does the pantomime.)

Use these verbs:

turn on the light   *wash out* (a shirt, etc.)
sit up   *put away* (a shirt, etc.)

stand up
put on a coat
plug in the toaster
let the cat *out*

hang up (a coat, etc.)
look at the newspaper
pick some books *up*

7. Answering Questions

Answer each question by completing the response or responses. In your answers, use the correct form of the two-word verb. Be ready to read your completed sentences aloud.

EXAMPLE: (turn on) What did Mrs. Jackson do to the light?

She _____*turned on*_____ the light.

She _*turned*_ it _*on*_____ .

1. (go off) What did the alarm clock do? It _____ at 6:30.

2. (put on) What kind of garment did Edna Jackson wear? She _____ a bathrobe.

3. (sit up) What did Mr. Jackson do? He _____ .

4. (plug in) What did Mrs. Jackson do to the coffee maker? She _____ the coffee maker. She _____ it _____ .

5. (use up) Why didn't she boil eggs? She had _____ the eggs yesterday. She had _____ them _____ yesterday.

6. (pop up) What does bread do after it is heated in some electric toasters? It _____ _____ .

7. (let out) What did Mrs. Jackson do to the cat? She _____ the cat _____ . She _____ it _____ .

8. (wash out) What did Jane forget to do last night? She forgot to _____ her clothes _____ . She forgot to _____ them _____ .

9. (have on) What did Jim ask his sister? He asked her what in the world she _____ _____ .

10. (run out of) What did Mrs. Jackson tell her children? She told them that she was _____ patience.

11. (put away) What did she tell Jane to do with her clothes? She said that Jane should _____ her clothes. She said that Jane should _____ them _____ .

12. (hang up) What else did she tell Jane? She said that Jane should _____ her clothes _____ . She said that Jane should _____ them _____ .

13. (care for) Did Edna Jackson _____ professional sports? No, she did not _____ them at all.

14. (let in) What did Mrs. Jackson do when the cat scratched outside the door? She _____ the cat _____ . She _____ it _____ .

15. (pick up) What did the twins do to their schoolbooks? They _____ their books. They _____ them _____ .

24

©1981 HBJ

8. Making Up Original Sentences

Turn back to this chapter's glossary. Make up an original sentence using ten of the two-word and three-word verbs. Your sentences should be about yourself or some people you know, not about the Jacksons. They may or may not be true.

EXAMPLES: My brother does not *care for* school.
I *came across* a book that he may like.

_____

_____

_____

_____

_____

_____

_____

_____

_____

_____

_____

_____

_____

_____

_____

_____

_____

_____

_____

3. Home Life (II)

What Is Going On in Mrs. Jackson's Busy Day?

George has gone to work, and the twins have gone to school. Edna dresses and then *tunes in* a news and music program on the radio. She listens while she works. She likes to know what is *going on* in the world.

Today Edna will not be working part-time in the library, as she usually does, so it is her day for cleaning. She *leaves* the radio *on* while she *cleans up* the kitchen. She *clears off* the table, *washes up* all the dirty dishes, and *wipes off* the table and the counters. She *washes out* the sink. She *rubs off* some stains from the stove top, where some soup *boiled over* when the twins were cooking yesterday. Then she *mops up* the kitchen floor.

Later Edna raises the windows in the bedrooms. She wants to *air* the rooms *out*. Soon she closes the windows to *shut out* the cold. Then she *puts up* clean curtains in one bedroom. She sees that the twins have *made up* the beds in their rooms. But she thinks, "Neither one of them has *put* any clothes *away* for three days!" In the bathroom she finds that the drain in the washbasin is *plugged up*. She tries to *open* it *up* with a plunger.

While she is *straightening up* the living room, the telephone rings. Cynthia Smith has *called up*. She wants Edna to become an officer of the League of Women Voters, in which Edna works actively. During the conversation the telephone suddenly becomes silent, and Edna *hangs up*. Cynthia soon *calls back*. "I believe that something *cut* us *off*," she says.

A little later Edna *sits down* to *make out* a menu for dinner and to prepare a shopping list. "The family *eats* everything *up* so fast," she thinks to herself. "Let's see. I need to *stock up on* sugar and flour and to buy some meat and vegetables for Saturday and Sunday. And we need eggs. This family doesn't like to *do without* eggs."

She does not *dress up* to go to the shopping center. She wears ordinary clothes. She goes into a clothing store and *tries on* some dresses but does not buy any. In the food store she *picks out* the vegetables and carefully *looks over* the meat.

Back home, she thinks, "I'd like to *lie down* and *doze off* for a few minutes, but it's too late. I'll have time only to mix a cake before I *cut up* the chicken."

GLOSSARY

INFINITIVE	PAST TENSE	PAST PARTICIPLE	

air . . . *out* . . .   **aired out**   [have] **aired out**   (S)

open windows or doors to let stale air out and fresh air in

We should *air out* this smoky room.

(Also I, receive fresh air: The room *aired out* quickly.

Similarly: The dirt *washed out* easily. The liquid *drained off* readily.)

boil *over*   **boiled over**   [have] **boiled over**   (I)

flow over the top (of a pan, etc.) while boiling

Part of the soup was lost when it *boiled over*.

call *back*   **called back**   [have] **called back**   (I)

call again (usually on the telephone)

George is not at home now. Can you *call back* later?

(Also S: Mr. Anderson *called* him *back* an hour later.)

call *up*   **called up**   [have] **called up**   (I)

call on the telephone (= British *ring up*)

Cynthia *called up* in the morning.

(Also S: She *called* me *up*.)

clean . . . *up* . . .   **cleaned up**   [have] **cleaned up**   (S)

make clean, remove dirt, etc.

Brendan *cleaned up* the garage floor.

(Also I: After working, he *cleaned up* by taking a shower.

He *cleaned* himself *up* in the bathroom.)

clear . . . *off* . . .   **cleared off**   [have] **cleared off**   (S)

remove dishes, etc., from

Jim helped Edna to *clear off* the table.

cut . . . *off* . . .   **cut off**   [have] **cut off**   (S)

stop, interrupt (concerning a telephone call)

The telephone company sometimes accidentally *cuts off* a call.

cut . . . *up* . . .   **cut up**   [have] **cut up**   (S)

cut into pieces

The recipe said to *cut up* the cabbage first.

do without _____   **did without**   [have] **done without**   (NS)

live without, manage without

The Jacksons *did without* heat when their furnace was broken.

(Also I: She had no butter, but she decided to *do without*.)

doze *off*   **dozed off**   [have] **dozed off**   (I)

begin to sleep

Jim *dozed off* but awoke suddenly.

dress *up*   **dressed up**   [have] **dressed up**   (I)

put on especially good or somewhat formal clothes

Many people *dress up* before going to church.

(Also S: She *dressed* the child *up* in her newest clothes.)

eat . . . *up* . . .   **ate up**   **[have] eaten up**   (S)
    eat, eat all of
        Have we *eaten up* the bread?

go *on*   **went on**   **[have] gone on**   (I)
    happen, occur (often in the form *going on*)
        Edna heard a noise and wondered what was *going on*.

hang *up*   (See Chapter 2)

leave . . . *on* . . .   **left on**   **[have] left on**   (S)
    allow to continue going or operating (a radio, television, record player, water,
    lights, etc.)
        Don't shut off the television yet. Please *leave* it *on*.

lie *down*   **lay down**   **[have] lain down**   (I)
    change to a lying position
        The cat was starting to *lie down* when she heard a dog.

look . . . *over* . . .   **looked over**   **[have] looked over**   (S)
    inspect, examine
        Good shoppers carefully *look over* everything they buy.

make . . . *out* . . .   **made out**   **[have] made out**   (S)
    think of and write (something short, such as a list)
        Edna sometimes *makes out* a list of things to do for the whole week.

make . . . *up* . . .   **made up**   **[have] made up**   (S)
    straighten bed covers or put fresh sheets on a bed
        "Do we have to *make up* our beds?" Jane and Jim asked.

mop . . . *up* . . .   **mopped up**   **[have] mopped up**   (S)
    clean (especially to clean a floor with a mop and water)
        The floor was dirty, so Edna *mopped* it *up*.

open . . . *up* . . .   **opened up**   **[have] opened up**   (S)
    cause to open (sometimes by removing an obstruction)
        The plumber *opened up* the drain.
        Billy *opened up* the package.
    (Also I, become open: The door *opens up* when he presses a button.)

pick . . . *out* . . .   **picked out**   **[have] picked out**   (S)
    select, choose
        The Jacksons *pick out* healthful foods.

plug . . . *up* . . .   **plugged up**   **[have] plugged up**   (S)
    close with dirt or hair or something else (*Block up* and *clog up* may have the
    same meaning.)
        Some paper had *plugged* the drain *up*.

put . . . *away* . . .   (See Chapter 2)

put . . . *up* . . .   **put up**   **[have] put up**   (S)
    hang (curtains or drapes) on rods or other fasteners
        The Jacksons *put up* new drapes in the living room.

rub . . . *off* . . .   **rubbed off**   **[have] rubbed off**   (S)
     remove by rubbing (moving a cloth, etc., while pressing down)
         Edna *rubbed off* a spot from her magazine cover.

shut . . . *out* . . .   **shut out**   **[have] shut out**   (S)
     exclude, keep out, lock out
         Some people put cotton into their ears to *shut out* loud noise.

sit *down*   **sat down**   **[have] sat down**   (I)
     change from a standing to a sitting position
         Ali *sat down* to read.

stock *up* on ____   **stocked up on**   **[have] stocked up on**   (NS)
     get a supply of, get a large amount for later use
         Edna *stocked up on* typing paper, which was on sale.
     (Also *stock up*: She needed typing paper, so she *stocked up*.)

straighten . . . *up* . . .   **straightened up**   **[have] straightened up**   (S)
     put into neat or proper order or condition
         The twins must learn to *straighten up* their own rooms.
     (Also I, become properly straight: The bushes *straightened up* after the storm.)

try . . . *on* . . .   **tried on**   **[have] tried on**   (S)
     put on a dress or other garment to judge its fit and appearance
         George *tried on* some new shoes, but they were too small.

tune . . . *in* . . .   **tuned in**   **[have] tuned in**   (S)
     turn (radio or television) controls so that the sound or picture is clear;
     choose a station or channel
         We tried to *tune in* Channel 8, but the picture was poor.
     (Also I: *Tune in* again tomorrow.)

wash . . . *out* . . .   **washed out**   **[have] washed out**   (S)
     wash the inside of (See also Chapter 2)
         Please *wash out* this pan for me.

wash . . . *up* . . .   **washed up**   **[have] washed up**   (S)
     wash, clean thoroughly (often by using water and soap)
         Joanna *washed up* the pans and spoons when she finished baking.

wipe . . . *off* . . .   **wiped off**   **[have] wiped off**   (S)
     clean the surface of (usually with a cloth, etc.)
         Fred *wiped off* some oil from his bicycle.

EXERCISES

1. Reading

Read "What Is Going On in Mrs. Jackson's Busy Day?" several times. Then perhaps each student may read a paragraph aloud.

2. Answering Questions

Answer each question by completing each response. The first part of the two-word verb is in parentheses, but you must choose the correct form. Be ready to read your completed sentences aloud.

1. (turn)   What does Edna do to the radio? She _____ the radio. She _____ it _____ .

2. (go)   Why does she listen to the news? She wants to know what is _____ .

3. (clean)   What does she do to the kitchen? She _____ the kitchen. She _____ it _____ .

4. (clear, wash, wipe, rub, mop)   She _____ the table _____ , _____ _____ the dishes, _____ the table, _____ _____ some stains on the stove top, and _____ the floor.

5. (leave)   What does she do to the radio while she is cleaning up the kitchen? She _____ the radio _____ . She _____ it _____ .

6. (boil)   What did the soup do yesterday? It _____ .

7. (air)   Why does Edna raise the bedroom windows? She wants to _____ the room.

8. (make)   Were the twins' beds neat? Yes. They had _____ them _____ . Yes. They had _____ their beds.

9. (hang)   What had the twins failed to do? They had not _____ their clothes.

10. (plug)   What is wrong with the bathroom drain? Some paper has _____ it _____ .

11. (open)   What does Edna do with the drain? She _____ the drain _____ with a plunger. She _____ it _____ with a plunger.

12. (straighten)   What does she do to the living room? She _____ the living room.

13. (call)   What does Cynthia Smith do? She _____ .

14. (call)   What does Cynthia do after the telephone suddenly becomes silent? She _____ .

15. (cut)   What does she say may have happened? She says that something _____ them _____ .

16. (sit)   Does Edna stand while she prepares a shopping list? No, she _____ .

17. (make)   How does she plan dinner? She _____ a menu.

18. (eat)   Do the Jacksons waste food? No. They _____ everything _____ quickly.

19. (stock)   What does Edna decide to get at the stores? She decides to _____ sugar and flour.

20. (do)   Do the Jacksons like eggs? Yes. They do not like to _____ eggs.

21. (dress)   Does Edna put on her best clothes when she goes shopping? No, she does not

_____ .

22. (try)   What does she do with some dresses in the shop? She _____ them _____ .

23. (pick, look)   What does she do to vegetables and fruit and meat? She _____ the vegetables and fruit and carefully _____ the meat.

24. (lie, doze)   What would she like to do at home? She would like to _____ and _____ .

25. (cut)   What does she do instead? She mixes a cake and _____ a chicken.

VERBS WITH "UP"

When *up* is used after some verbs, it mainly intensifies (makes stronger) the meaning. It also suggests that the action is finished, not just started. Often *up* may be omitted without changing the meaning very much. Here are the verbs from "Mrs. Jackson's Busy Day" that use *up* without changing the meaning greatly:

block up	make up (a bed)	clog up
eat up	wash up	plug up
straighten up	clean up	
call up	mop up	

Cleaning up a room, for example, is about the same as *cleaning* a room. *Making up* a bed is about the same as *making* a bed.

Other such verbs, some of which will appear in later chapters, are the following:

add up	burn up	count up
drink up	fill up	tie up
write up		

Sometimes *up* means a direction. When Edna *puts up* curtains, she really does move them *up* in front of the windows. *Climb up* and *move up* are other examples.

In a few words, *up* means "into small pieces":

break . . . **up** . . .	Robbers *broke up* some furniture.
chew . . . **up** . . .	The dog *chewed up* a small pillow.
chop . . . **up** . . .	George *chopped up* some wood.
cut . . . **up** . . .	Edna *cut* the chicken *up*.
tear . . . **up** . . .	The student *tore* his paper *up*.

Dress up does not have the same meaning as *dress*. It means "put on very good or rather formal clothes."

Most of the verbs listed are usually separable:

Edna *filled up* the dish.
Edna *filled* the dish *up*.

3. Using Verbs with "Up"

Read each of the following sentences aloud. Use first one of the parts in parentheses, then the other. If a blank is shown, add a similar word or words that you yourself think of.

1. Cynthia called (Edna, her friend, _____) up.

2. Edna cleaned up the (kitchen, bedroom, _____) yesterday.

3. Jane and Jim ate up (the candy, the eggs, _____) last night.

4. Edna made (the bed, the sofa) up.

5. She made out (a menu, a list of things she needed).

6. Mop (the basement floor, the kitchen floor) up, please.

7. The twins should straighten (their rooms, their desks, their _____) up.

8. Jane washed up (the dirty dishes, the pans, _____).

9. Some paper has plugged up (the sink, a drain).

10. The dog chewed up (a shoe, a small rug, _____).

11. Jane filled up (her glass, Jim's cup, _____).

12. Why did you tie (the dog, the box) up?

13. Did Edna cut up (the chicken, the oranges, the _____)?

14. Next, chop up (the eggs, the apples, _____).

15. Why did she tear up (the letter, the old dress, the _____)?

16. Who broke up (the furniture, the big piece of ice, _____)?

VERBS WITH "OFF" AND "OUT"

In the following verbs, *off* refers to the surface (the outer part) of something:

brush . . . **off** . . .	remove something with a brush or something similar
clear . . . **off** . . .	remove dishes from
dust . . . **off** . . .	take dust from the surface of
rinse . . . **off** . . .	wash lightly the surface of
rub . . . **off** . . .	remove by rubbing
wash . . . **off** . . .	wash the surface of
wipe . . . **off** . . .	clean the surface of

For example, when Edna *wipes off* the table, she wipes the surface of the table.

However, as the glossary shows, in telephone use to *cut off* is to stop or interrupt a call. To *doze off* is to begin to sleep.

In the following verbs, *out* refers to moving dust, etc., from the inside to the outside of something:

air . . . **out** . . .	move stale air from inside a room to outside
brush . . . **out** . . .	use a brush to move dirt, etc., from inside to outside
clean . . . **out** . . .	move dirt, etc., from inside to outside
rinse . . . **out** . . .	use water to move dirt, etc., from the inside
sweep . . . **out** . . .	use a broom to move dirt, etc., from inside
wash . . . **out** . . .	use water (and possibly soap, etc.) to move dirt, etc., from inside
wipe . . . **out** . . .	use a cloth, etc., to move dust, etc., from inside

Pick out, however, usually means "select, choose."

Edna *picks out* the food that she will cook.

Many of these verbs with *off* and *out* may have two kinds of objects. For example:

He brushed off the *table*.   (Names the surface that was brushed)
He brushed off the *snow*.   (Tells what was removed)

She rinsed out the *cup*.
She rinsed out the *tea leaves*.

4.   Using Verbs with "Off" and "Out"

Read each of the following sentences aloud. Use first one of the parts in parentheses, then the other. You or your teacher may then suggest some other possibilities.

1.   Edna rubbed off (some stains, some pencil marks).

2.   She brushed (the crumbs, some ants, the chair) off.

3.   Jane dusted off (the chair, her desk).

4.   George cleared (the table, the counter) off.

5.   Edna rinsed off (the plates, the spoons, the bits of food).

6.   Jim wiped (his bicycle, the dust) off.

7.   Edna washed off (the counter, some dried egg).

8.   Jim cleaned off (a shelf, several shelves, the rust).

9.   He also brushed out (the car, a large box, some spider webs).

10.   George cleaned out (a pail, the garage).

11.   He rinsed (an old pail, a pan) out.

12.   He washed out (an old pail, the pan, the white powder).

13.   He wiped (a pail, a pan) out.

14.   He swept out (the garage, one room, the dirt).

15.   Edna opened the doors to air (the room, the bedrooms) out.

5.   Making Up Pantomimes

For the following pantomimes two students may work together, then another two, and so on. Follow this example:

34

Student 1:   How do you mop up a floor?
Student 2:   This is the way to mop up a floor. (He or she pretends to mop up a floor.)
Student 1:   You mopped up that floor very well.

Use these verbs:

mop up a floor   *tear* a paper *up*
fill a glass *up*   *clear off* a table
make up a bed   *wipe off* a table
chop some wood *up*   *sweep* some dirt *out*
cut up an apple

6.   Making Up Original Sentences

Turn back to this chapter's glossary. Choose ten of the verbs that tell about something that you or some of your friends or relatives have done. Make a sentence with each.

EXAMPLES: I *aired out* my room because of the smoke.
My sister filled a pan too full, and it *boiled over*.

_____

_____

_____

_____

_____

_____

_____

_____

_____

_____

_____

_____

_____

_____

_____

_____

_____

_____

_____

4. Home Life (III)

The Jacksons Talk Things Over

When Jane and Jim *come **back*** from school, Jim says, "It's *clouding **up*** and *cooling **off***, Mom. I think a storm is *coming **up***."

"That's too bad," his mother answers. "I'd rather have it *warm **up***. I hate to see winter *set **in**.* I hope that a storm doesn't *snow* us ***in*** as it did last year. The snow was deep. We had to stay in the house for two days. If that happened now, I couldn't manage the special Book Fair at the library. So I hope it *clears **off**.*"

At the dinner table the Jacksons are more cheerful than they were during breakfast. Each person *puts **in*** a few comments about happenings of the day. Jane has read in school about some people on a boat who ***lived** on* raw fish for several weeks. Mr. Jackson says that a boiler *blew **up*** in the factory where he works. He *leaves **out*** the fact that his own life was in danger.

Jim *keeps **up*** the conversation by ***talking about*** the locker room in school. "We can't *shut **off*** one of the showers," he says, "so it ***keeps** on* running. It makes the whole room very wet and steamy. You have to *dry **off*** if you just walk through there."

Everyone helps with the dinner dishes. Then Mr. Jackson ***calls for*** the weekly family business conference. They ***talk about*** clothing especially. "I've *worn **out*** a pair of jeans," Jane says.

"I'm *growing **out** of* all my shirts," Jim says.

"I'd like a new dress," Mrs. Jackson comments, "but maybe I can *let **down*** the hem in my blue one."

George Jackson sighs and says, "I hate to ***part with*** this old jacket, but the elbows are pretty worn."

After *talking* the matter *over*, the Jacksons decide which clothes they can buy now.

Edna makes some calls about the Book Fair and then *sews **up*** some rips in the twins' clothing. George ***looks** at* television. The twins study and then play table tennis. The telephone *takes **up*** another half hour of each twin's time.

When the nightly news ends, George *turns **off*** the television. He *gets **up***, empties an ashtray, and says, "Well, folks, it's time to *turn **in**.*"

GLOSSARY

blow *up*   **blew up**   **[have] blown up**   (I)
    break apart suddenly and forcefully, explode, burst
        Another boiler has *blown up*.
    (Also S, cause to break apart suddenly: Soldiers *blew* the bridge *up*.)

***call* for ___**   **called for**   **[have] called for**   (NS)
    request, ask for
        The president *called for* peace.

clear *off*   **cleared off**   **[have] cleared off**   (I)
    become free of clouds (the sky) (often with *it* as the subject) (See also Chapter 3)
        It is *clearing off* rapidly.

cloud *up*   **clouded up**   **[have] clouded up**   (I)
    become cloudy (the sky) (often with *it* as the subject)
        It is *clouding up* and the wind is getting strong.

come *back*   **came back**   **[have] come back**   (I)
    return
        Fred *came back* because he had forgotten his coat.

come *up*   **came up**   **[have] come up**   (I)
    come near, approach, arrive (a storm)
        The snowstorm was *coming up* from the west.

cool *off*   **cooled off**   **[have] cooled off**   (I)
    become less warm, become cool
        The weather had started to *cool off*.
    (Also S, cause to become cool: The wind *cooled* us *off*.)

dry *off*   **dried off**   **[have] dried off**   (I)
    become less wet, become dry
        In the warm sun the wet grass *dried off* quickly.
    (Also S, cause (a thing or a person) to become dry: The sun *dried* the grass *off*.)

get *up*   (See Chapter 2)

grow *out* of ___   **grew out of**   **[have] grown out of**   (NS)
    become too big to wear (usually clothing or shoes)
        Small children *grow out of* their clothes very quickly.

***keep* on ___**   (See Chapter 2)

keep . . . *up* . . .   **kept up**   **[have] kept up**   (S)
    continue (usually with a noun or a pronoun as object)
        George hoped to *keep up* his work for many more years.

leave . . . *out* . . .   **left out**   **[have] left out**   (S)
    omit, not include, not say or do
        George *left out* part of the story.

let . . . *down* . . .	**let down**	**[have] let down**	(S)

lower (a hem in a garment), make a garment longer by making the hem narrower

Jane has not learned how to *let* a hem *down*.

live **on** ___	**lived on**	**[have] lived on**	(NS)

eat nothing except, exist with nothing but, subsist on

The sick man *lived on* chicken soup for a week.

look at ___   (See Chapter 2)

part **with** ___	**parted with**	**[have] parted with**	(NS)

give away or sell (something that one likes)

The Jacksons liked their old car but had to *part with* it.

put . . . *in* . . .   (See Chapter 1)

set *in*	**set in**	**[have] set in**	(I)

begin, start, commence (often a normal kind of change, as in the weather)

The rainy season was *setting in*.

sew . . . *up* . . .	**sewed up**	**[have] sewn** or **sewed up**	(S)

repair rips or holes in clothing with thread (pronounced sō, sōd, sōn)

This hole is too large. I can't *sew* it *up*.

shut . . . *off* . . .	**shut off**	**[have] shut off**	(S)

stop the water, gas, etc. (= *turn off*)

Please *shut off* the gas.

snow . . . *in* . . .	**snowed in**	**[have] snowed in**	(S)

keep in by deep snow

In Alaska some people are *snowed in* for weeks.

take . . . *up* . . .	**took up**	**[have] taken up**	(S)

use, occupy (time)

The business meeting *took up* twenty minutes.

talk **about** ___	**talked about**	**[have] talked about**	(NS)

consider, discuss, center a conversation or discussion on

Some people *talk about* things, some *talk about* people, and the wisest *talk about* ideas.

talk . . . *over* . . .	**talked over**	**[have] talked over**	(S)

consider what to do about, make an analysis of, discuss seriously and in detail

The Jacksons *talk over* important things together.

turn *in*	**turned in**	**[have] turned in**	(I)

go to bed, retire for the night (informal)

The Jacksons usually *turned in* after the news.

turn . . . *off* . . .   (See Chapter 2)

warm *up*	**warmed up**	**[have] warmed up**	(I)

become warm

The weather *warmed up* late in April.

(Also S, cause to become warm: Edna *warmed* the soup *up*.)

wear . . . *out* . . .   **wore out**   **[have] worn out**   (S)

make unusable by long wear or use, wear until ragged, wear or use as long as possible (usually clothing, shoes, machines, etc.)

These shoes are *worn out*. They have big holes in them.

(Also I, become unusable because of long wear or use: My coat *wore out*.
The tractor *wore out*.)

EXERCISES

1. Reading

Read "The Jacksons Talk Things Over" several times. Then each student may perhaps read a paragraph aloud.

2. Substituting

In the following sentences synonyms have been used for the two-word verbs. What two-word verb can be used instead of the italicized part of each sentence? Note that most of these sentences require past tense verbs. Be ready to read your sentences aloud.

1. Jim and Jane *returned* from school. (come) _____

_____

2. "It is *becoming cloudy* and *becoming cool*, Mom," Jim said. (cloud, cool) _____

_____

3. "I think a storm is *beginning to appear*," Jim added. (come) _____

_____

4. "I'd rather have it *become warmer*," Edna said. (warm) _____

_____

5. "I hate to see winter *begin*," Edna remarked. (set) _____

_____

6. "I hope that a storm doesn't *cause us to be kept in by snow*," Edna added. (snow) _____

_____

7. Edna hoped that it would *become free of clouds*. (clear) _____

_____

8. Each person *made* some comments on events of the day. (put) _____

_____

9. Jane told of some people who *existed with nothing but* raw fish for several weeks. (live) __

_____

10. George said that a boiler *broke apart suddenly and forcefully*. (blow) _____

_____

11. He *omitted* the fact that his own life had been in danger. (leave) _____

_____

12. Jim *continued* the conversation. (keep) _____

_____

13. He *discussed* incidents in the locker room. (talk) _____

_____

3. Substituting

Continue as in Exercise 2.

1. Jim said that students could not *stop the water* in one of the showers. (shut) _____

_____

2. "You have to *make yourself dry* after you just walk through there," he said. (dry) _____

_____

3. Mr. Jackson *requested* the weekly family meeting. (call) _____

_____

4. This time the family *discussed* clothing especially. (talk) _____

_____

5. Jane said, "I have *worn until they are unusable* one pair of jeans." (wear) _____

_____

6. "I have *grown too big to wear* my shirts," Jim said. (grow) _____

_____

7. Edna said, "Maybe I can *make* my blue dress *longer by making* the hem *narrower*." (let) (End
your sentence with *in my blue dress*.) _____

_____

8. George hated to *keep no longer* his old jacket. (part) _____

_____

9. After *considering what to do about* the matter, the Jacksons decided which new clothing they
could buy. (talk) _____

_____

10. Edna *repaired* some rips. (sew) _____

_____

11. The telephone *occupied* a half hour of Jim's time. (take) _____

_____

12. "Well, folks," Mr. Jackson said, "we should *go to bed* now." (turn) _____

_____

THE "-ING" FORM

Two- and three-word verbs, like other verbs, have forms ending in *-ing*. Examples:

It's *clouding up*.

42

It is *cooling off*.

A storm was *coming up*.

Jim kept up the conversation by *talking about* events at school.

Jim said, "I am *growing out of* all my clothes."

After *talking* the matter *over*, the Jacksons made a decision.

4. Using the "-ing" Form

Finish each of the following sentences by using the *-ing* form of the verb in parentheses.

1. (come back)   Jane and Jim were _____ from school.

2. (warm up)   The weather was not _____ .

3. (set in)   Winter was _____ .

4. (live on)   The shipwrecked people were _____ raw fish.

5. (keep up)   Jim is _____ the conversation _____ .

6. (talk about)   The members of the family are _____ ways to save money on their clothing.

7. (sew up)   Edna was _____ some rips in the twins' clothing.

8. (look at)   George was _____ television.

9. (turn off)   Now George is _____ the television.

10. (turn in)   The family will soon be _____ .

5. Using Past Participles

Each of the following sentences needs the past participle of the verb shown in parentheses. If you have forgotten the correct form, look again at the chapter's glossary.

EXAMPLE: (blow up)   The gasoline tank has ____*blown up*____ .

1. (blow up)   Two other tanks have _____ this year.

2. (come back)   The twins have not yet _____ .

3. (come up)   Another storm had _____ two days before.

4. (dry off)   Now the grass has _____ .

5. (grow out of)   Jim has _____ his shoes again.

6. (leave out)   George has _____ some important information.

7. (let down)   Edna has _____ several hems already.

8. (put in)   Jane has _____ several helpful suggestions.

9. (set in)   Winter has _____ earlier than usual this year.

10. (shut off)   The students have not _____ the water _____ .

11. (take up)   The discussions had _____ about an hour.

12. (wear out)   George had _____ his favorite jacket.

13. (live on) Many people have _____ rice or beans for a long time.

14. (cloud up) The sky has _____ again.

6. Trying Variations

Read each of the following sentences. Then think of another word (or group of words) that could also be used in each blank. Use your imagination if necessary.

EXAMPLE: (The boiler, _____*The tank*_____ , _____*The furnace*_____) may blow up.

1. (We, _____ , _____) came back early.

2. (The sidewalk, _____ , _____) soon dried off.

3. (The birds, _____ , _____) kept on coming.

4. The baby has grown out of its (shoes, _____ , _____).

5. Storm clouds (are, _____ , _____) coming up.

6. (I would not like to, _____) live on only one kind of food.

7. People are often sad when they must part with (an old dog, _____ , _____).

8. I enjoy talking about (the next hundred years, _____ , _____).

9. (This suit, _____ , _____) has worn out.

10. (The discussion, _____ , _____) took up too much time.

7. Making Up Original Sentences

Say some things about the weather using these verbs:

cloud up	come up	cool off
set in	snow . . . in . . .	warm up

_____

_____

_____

_____

_____

Say some things about talking, using these verbs:

call for ____	keep on ____	leave . . . out . . .
put . . . in . . .	talk about ____	talk . . . over . . .

_____

_____

_____

44

_____

_____

_____

Say some things about clothes, using these verbs:

dress up (Chapter 3)	wear . . . out . . . (Chapter 4)	sew . . . up . . . (Chapter 4)
hang . . . up . . . (Chapter 3)	grow out of ____ (Chapter 4)	pick . . . out . . . (Chapter 3)
let . . . down . . . (Chapter 4)	have . . . on . . . (Chapter 2)	put . . . away . . . (Chapter 2)
put . . . on . . . (Chapter 2)	part with ____ (Chapter 4)	wash . . . out . . . (Chapter 3)

_____

_____

_____

_____

_____

_____

_____

_____

_____

_____

_____

5. Personal Relationships (I)

Getting Along Together

Helen and Maria shared an apartment near State University. Their friends, Tom and Pedro, *showed up* there two or three times each week. All four of them *got along* very well.

One evening Tom and Pedro wanted to *come over*. Pedro asked on the telephone, "May we *drop in* for a few minutes?"

When they arrived, Tom knocked on the door. "*Come in*," said Helen.

A little later, Pedro said, "I wanted to tell you that I *bumped into* Don Powell today."

"Oh," Maria said. "Did you *find out* whether he and Susan Peterson *made up*?"

"Yes. You remember that she *walked out on* him. She couldn't *put up with* his bad temper. But now they have *made up* and are good friends again. They and a couple named Bill and Wanda may *team up* in operating a little ice cream shop."

"I *ran across* Susan yesterday," Maria said. "She told me that she would *look in on* us soon."

"Oh, did you *run into her*, too?" Tom asked. "I saw her last week. She has a part-time job in a store downtown. She was *waiting on* some other customers." He grinned teasingly at Helen. "She's very bright. I think I'll *ask* her *out* sometime."

"We could all *take* her *out*," Helen said. "She works too hard. She's easy to *warm up to*, as she's very sweet and never tries to *show off*. We should *take* her *away* from her job and her books for a few hours. I hope that she and Don will both *stop by*."

"You have good ideas, Helen," said Tom. "Maybe the four of us and Don and Susan and their new friends can *get together* soon for a party or a picnic. Should we *wait for* them to call, or shall we *bring up* the idea ourselves?"

"Let's call them. Shall I *call up* Susan right now?" Maria asked. "If they are too busy, she can simply *turn us down*, or maybe we'll need to *put off* the get-together for a while."

GLOSSARY

INFINITIVE	PAST TENSE	PAST PARTICIPLE	
ask...*out*...	**asked out**	[**have**] **asked out**	(S)

invite (usually a person of the opposite sex) to go with one (usually to a
dinner, dance, party, movie, etc.)
> Lee *asked* Betty *out.* They went to dinner and a movie.

bring...*up*...	**brought up**	[**have**] **brought out**	(S)

propose, suggest
> Who *brought up* such a topic to discuss?

bump **into** ___	**bumped into**	[**have**] **bumped into**	(NS)

meet by chance (similar to but less formal than *run into* and *run across*)
> Where did Pedro *bump into* Don Powell?

call . . . *up* . . .   (See Chapter 3)

come *in*	**came in**	[**have**] **come in**	(I)

enter
> The boys *came in* as soon as Helen opened the door.

come *over*	**came over**	[**have**] **come over**	(I)

come, come to one's home (or office, etc.)
> Why don't you and Pedro *come over?*

drop *in*	**dropped in**	[**have**] **dropped in**	(I)

come to visit briefly (often without first calling or writing) (= *stop by, look in on*)
> Who *dropped in* at the girls' apartment?

find . . . *out* . . .   (See Chapter 1)

get *along*	**got along**	[**have**] **got** or **gotten along**	(I)

live as friends, be friendly with one another, agree in many opinions and attitudes
(See also Chapter 1)
> Some married couples *get along* better than others.

get *together*	**got together**	[**have**] **got** or **gotten together**	(I)

come together as a pair or as a group, meet (usually informally)
> Did the eight students ever *get together?*

look *in* **on** ___	**looked in on**	[**have**] **looked in on**	(NS)

come to see, come to visit briefly (= *drop in, stop by*)
> "Let's *look in on* Maria and Helen this evening," Tom suggested.

make *up*	**made up**	[**have**] **made up**	(I)

become friends again, end a quarrel (for *make* . . . *up* . . . see Chapter 1)
> Have Don and Susan *made up* since their argument?

put . . . *off* . . .   (See Chapter 1)

put *up* **with** ___	**put up with**	[**have**] **put up with**	(NS)

accept (a situation that one does not like), tolerate, bear patiently
> Some students have to *put up with* roommates that they do not like.

run across ____   **ran across**   **[have] run across**   (NS)
    happen to find or meet (= *run into*, *bump into*)
        Where did Tom *run across* Susan?

***run* into** ____   ran into   **[have] run into**   (NS)
    happen to find or meet (similar to *run across*)
        Who else *ran into* Susan?

show *off*   **showed off**   **[have] shown** or **showed off**   (I)
    display boastfully (one's good qualities, appearance, ability, etc.), make a show of
        Do you like people who *show off*?

show *up*   **showed up**   **[have] shown** or **showed up**   (I)
    come, appear, arrive (often when not expected)
        Has Bill *shown up* yet?

stop *by*   **stopped by**   **[have] stopped by**   (I)
    come to visit briefly (often without first calling or writing) (= *drop in*, *look in on*)
        Will Andy and Pedro *stop by* again today?

take . . . *away* . . .   **took away**   **[have] taken away**   (S)
    steal, deprive (someone) of (something), remove
        Sally is afraid that Roy may *take away* a book she needs.

take . . . *out* . . .   **took out**   **[have] taken out**   (S)
    take (often someone of the opposite sex) to a meal or other social occasion
        Did Jack ever *take* Susan *out*?

team *up*   **teamed up**   **[have] teamed up**   (I)
    work together (often followed by *with*)
        Have Tom and Sam ever *teamed up* against other tennis players?
        Yes, Tom often *teams up* with Sam.

turn . . . *down* . . .   **turned down**   **[have] turned down**   (S)
    refuse, decline, not accept (an invitation)
        Will Susan and Don *turn* the invitation *down*?

***wait* for** ____   **waited for**   **[have] waited for**   (NS)
    stay until (someone) comes, await or expect (someone or something)
        Fred *waited for* Rachel to open the door.

***wait* on** ____   **waited on**   **[have] waited on**   (NS)
    serve, try to fill the needs of (a customer) (Also: *wait upon* ____)
        People who *wait on* others should be pleasant.

walk *out* on ____   **walked out on**   **[have] walked out on**   (NS)
    go away from, desert, leave, part company with (informal)
        Did Don *walk out on* Susan?

warm *up* to ____   **warmed up to**   **[have] warmed up to**   (NS)
    become friendly toward, have good feelings about (informal)
        Did Helen *warm up to* Susan?

EXERCISES

1. Reading

Read "Getting Along Together" several times. Be ready to read any part of it aloud.

2. Answering Questions

Answer each question by completing each response. Use the same verb that is used in the question, but change its form if necessary. (One student may read the question, another the answer.)

1. Who *showed up* at Helen and Maria's apartment? Tom and Pedro _____ .

2. Do Tom, Pedro, Helen, and Maria *get along* well? Yes, they _____ very well.

3. Did Tom and Pedro *come over* to the girls' apartment? Yes, they _____ one evening last week.

4. Did Pedro ask whether they might *drop in*? Yes. He said, "May we _____ for a few minutes?"

5. Whom had Pedro *bumped into*? He had _____ Don Powell.

6. Did Don and Susan *make up* after their quarrel? Yes, they _____ .

7. Had Susan *walked out on* Don? Yes, she had _____ him.

8. Would Susan *put up with* Don's bad temper? No, she would not _____ it.

9. With whom did Susan and Don *team up* in business? They _____ with Bill and Wanda.

10. Who *ran across* Susan yesterday? It was Maria who _____ Susan.

11. Did Susan say that she would *look in on* Helen and Maria? Yes, she promised to _____ them.

12. Who else had *run into* Susan? Tom had _____ her last week.

3. Answering Questions

Continue as in Exercise 2.

1. Did Susan *wait on* Tom when he was in the store? No, she was _____ other customers.

2. Did Tom say that he might *ask* Susan *out*? Yes, he told his friends that he might _____ her _____ .

3. Did Helen also want to *take* Susan *out*? She thought that all four of them should _____ her _____ .

4. Isn't it easy to *warm up to* Susan? Helen said that it is easy to _____ her.

5. Who did Helen hope would *stop by*? She hoped that Susan and Don would _____ .

6. Who might *get together* for a picnic or a party? Tom thought that the eight young people might _____ .

7. Did Tom want to *wait for* Susan to call? He asked whether they should _____ her and Don to call.

8. Did Tom always expect others to *bring up* suggestions for parties? No, he sometimes _____ them _____ himself.

9. Did Maria *call up* Susan? She probably _____ her _____ .

10. Did Susan *turn* the invitation *down*? We do not know whether or not she _____ it _____ .

11. Did the students *put off* the party or picnic? Maybe they did _____ it _____ .

QUESTIONS WITH TWO-WORD VERBS

Questions with two-word verbs are like other questions in English.

Yes-no questions can be answered by *yes* or *no*. They usually start with forms of *be, have, do, may, can, shall, will,* or *must.*

Are you *waiting for* someone?	(Yes, I am.)
Did Tom *ask* Susan *out*?	(No, he didn't.)
Have Don and Susan *made up*?	(Yes, they have.)

Wh- questions usually ask for information about who(m), what, when, where, why, or how.

Who *ran across* Susan?	(Maria did.)
Whom° did Tom *run across*?	(He *ran across* Susan.)
What wouldn't Susan *put up with*?	(She wouldn't *put up with* Don's bad temper.)
When are Tom and Pedro *coming over*?	(They are *coming over* this evening.)
Where will Tom and Pedro *show up* next?	(I don't know.)
Why should Maria *call up* Susan?	(She wants to plan a party.)
How do the four students *get along*?	(Very well.)
What question has Tom *brought up*?	(He wonders whether or not there can be a party.)

°Informal English uses *who* in sentences like this.

Verb Forms Generally Used After Helping Verbs in Questions

After these helping verbs:	Generally use this form:
be (am, is, are, was, were, been)	-ING Are they *getting* along well? Is Dave *showing* off? Why was Dave *showing* off?
do (does, did) may (might) can (could) shall (should) will (would) must	SIMPLE FORM Did Pedro *run* into Don? May Tom and Pedro *drop* in? When will the eight students *get* together? Who could *turn* down that invitation?
have (has, had)	PAST PARTICIPLE Has Pedro *found* out anything new? Have Pedro and Tom *shown* up yet? Why has Tom *come* over?

---

4. Asking "Yes-No" Questions

Change each of these statements into a *yes-no* question. The first word of the question is given. Use the correct form of the italicized verb. In writing, put a question mark at the end of each sentence.

EXAMPLE: Helen is *waiting for* someone.   *Is Helen waiting for someone?*

1. Tom and Pedro are *coming over*.   Are _____

   _____

2. Susan and Don *made up*.   Did _____

   _____

3. Susan and Don have *made up*.   Have _____

   _____

4. Tom *ran into* Susan.   Did _____

   _____

5. Susan never tries to *show off*.   Is _____

   _____

6. We should *wait for* our friends to come.   Should _____

   _____

7. We can *get together* for a picnic. <u>Can</u> _____

_____

8. Maria *calls* Susan *up*. <u>Does</u> _____

_____

9. The friends have *put off* the party. <u>Have</u> _____

_____

10. Susan and Don *turned* us *down*. <u>Did</u> _____

_____

11. Nations, like people, can *make up* when they disagree. <u>Can</u> _____

_____

12. National leaders should *bring up* new ideas for a peaceful world. <u>Should</u> _____

_____

13. Nations can *get along* together. <u>Can</u> _____

_____

14. Nations should *team up* to fight hunger and disease. <u>Should</u> _____

_____

15. All of us must *put up with* the "strange" customs and beliefs of other countries. <u>Must</u> _____

_____

5. Asking "Wh-" Questions

Change each of these statements into a *wh-* question. The first word or words are given. Use the italicized verb in your question.

EXAMPLE: Thursday evening Susan *looked in on* Helen and Maria.
When did *Susan look in on Helen and Maria?* _____

1. Tom and Pedro *showed up* at Helen and Maria's apartment last night. <u>When</u> _____

_____

2. They *show up* there two or three times each week. <u>How often</u> _____

_____

3. Tom *ran into* Susan in a store downtown. <u>Where</u> _____

_____

4. Tom *ran into* Susan. <u>Who</u> _____

_____

5. Tom *ran into* Susan in a store. <u>Whom did</u> _____

_____

6. Susan was *waiting on* other customers. Whom was Susan _____
_____

7. The eight students *got together* for a picnic on Saturday. When did _____
_____

8. Susan and Don are *coming over* tonight. When _____
_____

9. Don may *put off* the party. Who _____
_____

10. Don may *put off* the party. What _____
_____

11. Susan and Don *stopped by* yesterday. When did _____
_____

12. Bill and Wanda also *dropped in*. Who else _____
_____

13. They *stopped by* to talk about the picnic. Why did _____
_____

14. Helen and Tom *get along* well. How do _____
_____

15. Helen and Tom *get along* well because they like each other. Why do _____
_____

6. Making Up Original Sentences

Turn back to this chapter's glossary. Choose at least ten of the verbs and make an original sentence with each. Your sentences should be about yourself or someone you know. Then change each sentence into a question.

      EXAMPLE: My best friend *came over* last night.
                   Who *came over* last night?

_____

_____

_____

_____

_____

_____

6. Personal Relationships (II)

An Old Man Looks Back On His Life

Mr. Jackson's father had just *passed away*. He had died of cancer. George had *sat up with* him during the last night at the hospital. Both men knew that the end was *drawing near*, but the older man *kept on* talking cheerfully.

"I am not unhappy," he told his son. "Sometimes life has been difficult, but I usually *faced up to* its problems. When I was a student, I *tried out for* the football team and didn't *meet with* success. I *dropped out of* high school for a year after that. I *fell in with* some young men who were robbing people on the streets. We didn't use real guns. We *held* people *up* with wooden guns that looked real.

"The police arrested five of us and made us *line up* at the station. They *called in* people who had been robbed and asked them to *pick out* the robber. The boy who had done most of the robbing was not there. He had *gotten away*.

"One of the people *picked out* another boy and me, but of course we didn't *let on* that we were guilty. I promised myself that if I *got out of* trouble, I'd *go back* to school and never steal again. I've never *gone back on* that promise.

"I *met with* a lawyer several times, and at the trial the judge *let* me *off* with a warning. Back in school I worked hard and graduated, and then I *looked for* a job. A couple of years later I met your mother and we really *fell for* each other. I was ready to *settle down*, and we got married.

"Your mother always *stood by* me, even when times were hard and food was scarce. When I needed help, she always gave it to me. She never *hung back*. She was a wonderful woman, George. I *look back on* our years of marriage with no regrets. Sara and I always *pulled together* like a team of— a team of—a team of good horses."

He was getting tired and was beginning to *drift off*, but he tried to keep talking. His son could hardly *hold back* the tears.

"She was a—was a wonderful—wonderful . . . ." The old man's voice faded, and his breathing suddenly stopped. George *rang for* the nurse.

GLOSSARY

INFINITIVE	PAST TENSE	PAST PARTICIPLE	
call . . . *in* . . .	**called in**	**[have] called in**	(S)

ask (someone) to come to a place
The police *called in* the people who had been robbed.

draw *near*	**drew near**	**[have] drawn near**	(I)

come close, approach
The time *drew near* for the doctor to come in.

drift *off*	**drifted off**	**[have] drifted off**	(I)

become unconscious, go to sleep; (of the voice) become indistinct
His voice *drifted off* as weariness overcame him.

drop *out of* _____	**dropped out of**	**[have] dropped out of**	(NS)

stop going to or participating in (often a school or a contest)
Dropping out of school is usually not wise.

face *up to* _____	**faced up to**	**[have] faced up to**	(NS)

meet boldly, oppose strongly, admit the difficulty or danger of
George's father *faced up to* many problems.

fall **for** _____	**fell for**	**[have] fallen for**	(NS)

become very fond of, begin to love, fall in love with (informal)
He *fell for* a girl in his class at school.

fall *in* **with** _____	**fell in with**	**[have] fallen in with**	(NS)

join, happen to meet or associate with (bad companions)
The boy *fell in with* some young robbers.

get *away*	**got away**	**[have] got or gotten away**	(I)

escape, become free of whatever is holding one
One robber *got away* by swimming across the river.

get *out of* _____	**got out of**	**[have] got or gotten out of**	(NS)

become free of, go out from, escape from, leave
The boy hoped that he could *get out of* trouble.

go *back*	**went back**	**[have] gone back**	(I)

return (Many other two-word verbs may mean "return": *come back, drive back, hurry back,* etc.)
Later he was glad that he had *gone back* to school.

go *back* **on** _____	**went back on**	**[have] gone back on**	(NS)

fail to keep (a promise), not do what one has agreed to do
"Always do what you promise," he once told George. "Never *go back on* your word."

hang *back*	**hung back**	**[have] hung back**	(I)

be unwilling to go forward
People who are afraid often *hang back*.

hold . . . *back* . . .   **held back**   **[have] held back**   (S)
> keep back, keep (someone or something) from moving, prevent (someone from doing something)
>> The police could hardly *hold back* the crowd.

hold . . . *up* . . .   **held up**   **[have] held up**   (S)
> rob (often with a gun or other weapon), stop by force and rob
>> Two robbers *held up* a small store on the north side of town.

keep . . . *on* . . .   (See Chapter 2)

let . . . *off* . . .   **let off**   **[have] let off**   (S)
> allow to go free or unpunished
>> Some judges will not *let off* young criminals; they make them go to prison.

let *on* ____   **let on**   **[have] let on**   (NS)
> allow it to be known, admit (usually followed by a clause starting with *that*) (informal)
>> Billy didn't *let on* that he was hurt.

line *up*   **lined up**   **[have] lined up**   (I)
> form a line, stand in line, get into a line (= British *queue up*)
>> About a hundred people *lined up* in front of the theater.

look *back* on ____   **looked back on**   **[have] looked back on**   (NS)
> remember, recall, think about (past events)
>> Mr. Jackson *looked* happily *back on* his life.

***look* for ____**   (See Chapter 1)

***meet* with ____**   **met with**   **[have] met with**   (NS)
> come together with (usually to discuss a serious matter); encounter
> (often followed by *success* or *failure*)
>> The boy *met with* his lawyer several times.
>> They *met with* success.

pass *away*   **passed away**   **[have] passed away**   (I)
> die (generally used only to refer to a friend or a relative)
>> George's mother had *passed away* three years earlier.

pick . . . *out* . . .   **picked out**   **[have] picked out**   (S)
> identify from a group (See also Chapter 3)
>> Try to *pick out* the two oldest people in this picture.

pull *together*   **pulled together**   **[have] pulled together**   (I)
> work together, cooperate
>> In a good marriage the husband and wife *pull together*.

***ring* for ____**   **rang for**   **[have] rung for**   (NS)
> call by using a bell or buzzer
>> If a person in a hospital is in unusual pain, he or she may *ring for* a nurse.

settle *down*   **settled down**   **[have] settled down**   (I)
> begin to lead a regular life, start a home or family
>> Most young people *settle down* in their twenties.

sit *up* **with** _____   **sat up with**   **[have] sat up with**   (NS)

    stay with (especially at night and with a person who is ill)

       In many countries friends or relatives *sit up with* sick people.

stand *by* _____   **stood by**   **[have] stood by**   (NS)

    remain loyal to, work with, help even when someone is in trouble

       Good friends will always *stand by* you.

try *out* **for** _____   **tried out for**   **[have] tried out for**   (NS)

    attempt to become part of (a team or any activity in which certain skills are needed)

       In schools many students *try out for* an athletic team or a musical group.

EXERCISES

1. Reading

Read "An Old Man Looks Back On His Life" several times. Be ready to read any part of it aloud.

2. Substituting

In the following sentences synonyms have been used for the two-word and three-word verbs. What two- or three-word verb could be used instead of the italicized part of each sentence? Use the correct form. Read the new sentences aloud.

1. Mr. Jackson's father had just *died*.   (pass) _____

   _____

2. His voice *became indistinct* as he was losing consciousness.   (drift) _____

   _____

3. George had *stayed with* him during the past night.   (sit) _____

   _____

4. Both men had known that the end was *approaching*.   (draw) _____

   _____

5. "I always *met boldly* all of life's problems," the old man said.   (face) _____

   _____

6. When I was a student, I *attempted to become a member of* the football team.   (try) _____

   _____

7. I *stopped attending* school for a year.   (drop) _____

   _____

8. I *happened to associate with* some young criminals.   (fall) _____

   _____

9. We *stopped* people *by force and robbed* them.   (hold)   (Delete *them*.) _____

   _____

10. The police arrested five of us and made us *form a line* at the police station.   (line) _____

    _____

11. They *asked* people who had been robbed *to come* to the station.   (call) _____

    _____

12. They wanted them to *identify* the robber.   (pick) _____

    _____

13. The boy who had done most of the robbing *escaped*. (get) _____

_____

14. Another boy and I didn't *allow it to be known* that we were guilty. (let) _____

_____

15. I promised myself that if I *became free of* this trouble, I would never rob anyone else. (get)

_____

3. Substituting

Continue as in Exercise 2.

1. The old man began speaking again. "I said that I would *return* to school." (go) _____

_____

2. I did not *fail to keep* that promise. (go) _____

_____

3. I *came together with* a lawyer several times. (meet) _____

_____

4. At the trial the judge *allowed* me *to go free* with a warning. (let) _____

_____

5. After I graduated, I *tried to find* a job. (look) _____

_____

6. A girl and I *became very fond of* each other a couple of years later. So we got married. (fall)

_____

7. I was ready to *lead a regular life*. (settle) _____

_____

8. Your mother always *was loyal to* me, even in trouble. (stand) _____

_____

9. She never *was unwilling to go forward*. (hang) _____

_____

10. I *remember* our years of marriage with no regrets. (look) _____

_____

11. Sara and I always *cooperated* like a team of good horses. (pull) _____

_____

12. The old man could hardly talk any more, and George could hardly *prevent* the tears. (hold)

_____

13. He *called* the nurse *by using a bell*. (ring) _____

_____

THREE-WORD VERBS

The three-word verbs in this chapter are:

drop out of ____	get out of ____	sit up with ____
face up to ____	go back on ____	try out for ____
fall in with ____	look back on ____	

In Chapters 1–5 you have already studied these three-word verbs:

brush up on ____ (Chapter 1)	let ____ in on ____ (Chapter 2)	stock up on ____ (Chapter 3)
catch up with ____ (Chapter 1)	look in on ____ (Chapter 5)	try . . . out . . . on ____ (Chapter 1)
grow out of ____ (Chapter 4)	put up with ____ (Chapter 5)	walk out on ____ (Chapter 5)
keep up with ____ (Chapter 1)	run out of ____ (Chapter 2)	warm up to ____ (Chapter 5)

Answer these questions:

1. In saying three-word verbs aloud, which word is always pronounced a little more strongly than the other two?_____

_____

2. With two exceptions, where should the object of each of these three-word verbs be placed?_____

_____

3. One exception is *let* ____ *in on* ____ , as in this sentence: Jane *let* Jim *in on* a secret. Notice that there are two objects in that sentence. What are those objects?_____

_____

4. The other exception is *try . . . out . . . on* ____ , as in these sentences: (a) Jane *tried out* an idea *on* Jim. (b) Jane *tried* it *out on* Jim. In (a) the objects follow which two parts of the verb? In (b) they follow which two parts? So, in this unusual three-word verb, there are two objects, and the first of them may be before or after *out*._____

_____

4. Pronouncing Three-Word Verbs

One student may read each sentence aloud, including the expression printed inside the parentheses. Then one or more students may think of other expressions that will fit there and read the sentence with them. (This can be a written exercise if the teacher prefers.)

EXAMPLE: Is it wise to *drop out of* (a class, *school* , *the band*)?

1. Everyone must *face up to* (problems, _____).

2. Some good young people *fall in with* (bad ones, _____).

3. The girl wanted to *get out of* (the class, _____).

4. A man should not *go back on* (what he believes, _____).

5. Almost everyone has (some happy days, _____ , _____ ____ , _____) to *look back on.*

6. In the past, (relatives, _____) usually *sat up with* anyone who was seriously ill.

7. Students may *try out for* (a musical group, _____).

8. In reviewing algebra, Tom *brushed up on* (the first four chapters, _____).

9. Brendan *caught up with* (Helen, _____ , _____).

10. Pedro walked so fast that (the girls, _____ , _____) could hardly *keep up with* him.

11. The teacher *tried out* a new kind of lesson *on* (two students, _____).

12. The teacher *tried it out on* (only one class, _____).

13. Please *let* (me, _____ , _____) *in on* the secret.

14. We *ran out of* (gasoline, _____ , _____).

15. Edna Jackson *stocked up on* (potatoes, _____ , _____ , _____).

16. Small children quickly *grow out of* (their shoes, _____ , _____).

17. Let's *look in on* (our friends, _____ , _____).

18. It's hard to *put up with* (cold weather, _____ , _____ , _____).

19. Sometimes a married man *walks out on* (his family, _____).

20. Most persons cannot easily *warm up to* (people who are not pleasant, _____).

5. Using Three-Word Verbs

Complete each sentence by choosing the most suitable three-word verb from this list:

catch up with ____	get out of ____	run out of ____
drop out of ____	go back on ____	sit up with ____
face up to ____	look back on ____	stock up on ____
fall in with ____	put up with ____	try out for ____

1. Have you enough bread and milk, Mrs. Smith?
   There's enough bread, Maria, but I have _____ milk.

2. Should I bring you some rice from the store?
   Yes, I would like to _____ rice.

3. May I bring you some vegetables, too?
   Yes, please. I would like to have food here when Jack _____ jail.

4. Why does Jack have so much trouble?
   He often _____ friends who are criminals.

5. Did he stay in school?
   No, he _____ school last year.

6. Did he play basketball in school?
   He _____ the basketball team.

7. Did the coach like the way Jack played?
   Yes, but he would not _____ Jack's bad temper.

8. When Jack is a little older, maybe he will be better.
   I hope so. He must learn to _____ responsibilities.

9. I believe that Jack is really an honest boy.
   Yes. He never _____ a promise.

10. Perhaps some day he will settle down.
    I believe that he will. Then I can _____ this year and think that it was only a bad dream.

11. Mrs. Smith, I see my husband starting out for work. If I hurry, I can _____ him.

12. Thanks for _____ me last night when I was sick, Maria. You are a good friend.

6. Completing Sentences

Finish each sentence by adding the missing word. If possible, do so without looking again at the glossary.

1. His last hours were quiet, and he passed _____ without pain.

2. One young robber was not caught. He got _____ .

3. Many college students go _____ to their home towns after they graduate.

4. The teacher told the children to line _____ in a straight row.

5. Ella lost her ring. She looked _____ it in every room.

6. It is natural for a young man and a young woman to fall _____ each other.

7. If you need help, just ring _____ it.

8. A good friend will stand _____ you when you are in trouble.

9. A man and wife should be like a team of good horses. They should pull _____ .

10. George Jackson's father got into trouble as a young man, but he finally settled _____ .

11. After a house has been robbed, one should call _____ the police to try to find the robber.

12. Three boys held _____ a filling station, but they were caught by the police.

13. Some judges let young criminals _____ if they have not been arrested before.

14. When a holiday draws _____ , children are usually excited.

15. Parents must sometimes hold children _____ to keep them away from danger.

16. George had heard his father's stories before, but he did not let _____ that he had.

17. Parents sometimes meet _____ teachers to talk about children's schoolwork.

18. My dog did not want to go across the bridge with me. It kept hanging _____ .

19. She seemed more and more tired and sleepy. Soon she would drift _____ .

20. Here are several apples. Pick _____ the two that are the largest.

7. Making Up Original Sentences

Pick out at least ten of the two-word verbs in this chapter's glossary and write an original sentence with each.

_____

_____

_____

_____

_____

_____

_____

_____

_____

_____

_____

_____

_____

_____

_____

_____

_____

_____

7. Transportation and Travel

The Jacksons Set Out on a Trip

The Jackson family **got into** their car and *set out* to spend Christmas with Mrs. Jackson's mother and father. Tom, who was at home for the holidays, was driving. He *headed out* toward the highway. The neighbors' dog *saw* them *off*; he was running and barking.

Tom had to *turn around* almost at once, however, because the twins had forgotten their present for their grandparents. After they *got **back*** to the house, Jane *got out* to find the missing package. She *got **in*** again, and Tom *backed out* of the driveway. Again they were on their way.

Edna was reminded of her last trip to visit her parents, when she had gone in an airplane. "We *checked in* early at the airport," she told the children, "and I *got on* without waiting long. But the plane didn't *take off* for another hour and a half. Your father *sent* me *off* with a big bouquet, but the flowers were already wilting before we left the ground. The flight was smooth and pleasant, though. I heard the noise when the pilot *let* the wheels ***down*** in Springfield, and we ***headed into*** the unloading area without any trouble. As soon as I ***got off*** the plane, I saw Grandma and Grandpa. We *dined **out*** at a lovely restaurant before we went to their house."

A driver *cut **in*** ahead of them. They could see him *weaving in and out* among the cars ahead. "He must be drunk," said Mr. Jackson. The driver ***ran off*** the road, ***ran over*** a pile of sand beside the road, and ***plowed into*** a parked truck. Tom *pulled over* and stopped to see whether the driver was hurt. The Jacksons stayed there for a few minutes until a policeman *came up*.

After a couple of hours the Jacksons had trouble of their own. Mr. Jackson was saying, "This car is old. I hope that it doesn't *break **down*** before we get there." Just then the right front tire *blew **out***. Everybody *piled out*. Jim *jacked **up*** the front end, Tom *took off* the tire, and Jim *put* the spare tire *on*. "I didn't ***figure on*** a blowout," said Mr. Jackson.

They had no more trouble, and they *pulled **in*** at the grandparents' house only an hour late.

GLOSSARY

back *out*   **backed out**   **[have] backed out**   (I)
    drive (a car, etc.) backward from a place
        Ahmed *backed out* carefully.
    (Also S: Tom *backed* the car *out* carefully.)

blow *out*   **blew out**   **[have] blown out**   (I)
    burst, lose air suddenly (a tire)
        A rear tire *blew out.*

break *down*   **broke down**   **[have] broken down**   (I)
    stop working, stop running or operating (an automobile or other machine)
        Most machines *break down* sometimes.

check *in*   **checked in**   **[have] checked in**   (I)
    arrive and register at (a hotel, airport, etc.)
        When you reach your hotel, you should *check in* at once.

come *up*   **came up**   **[have] come up**   (I)
    arrive (usually by chance) (See also Chapter 4)
        A policeman *came up* and asked some questions.

cut *in*   **cut in**   **[have] cut in**   (I)
    move suddenly in front of (a driver or a vehicle)
        Good drivers do not *cut in.*

dine *out*   **dined out**   **[have] dined out**   (I)
    eat dinner in a (usually expensive) restaurant (*Eat out* may be used for any
    meal and for any sort of restaurant.)
        The Jacksons seldom *dine out* because of the high prices.

***figure* on _____**   **figured on**   **[have] figured on**   (NS)
    expect (informal)
        Do not *figure on* meeting only good drivers.

get *back*   **got back**   **[have] got** or **gotten back**   (I)
    arrive at the place where one started, return
        The Jacksons *got back* two days after Christmas.

get *in*   **got in**   **[have] got** or **gotten in**   (I)
    enter (a car, etc.) (When the verb has an object, *get into* is used instead of *get in*.
    See also the note below under *get into.*)
        They went to their car and *got in.*

***get* into _____**   **got into**   **[have] got** or **gotten into**   (NS)
    enter (a car, etc.) Note that people *get into* a car or a small plane, but they
    get on a large plane or a bus, train or horse. See also Chapter 2. *Get into* may also
    refer to a game, trouble, an argument, etc.)
        They walked out and *got into* their car.
        We *got into* a game of backgammon (trouble, a quarrel).

get *off*   **got off**   **[have] got** or **gotten off**   **(I)**

    leave (a plane, bus, train, or horse)

        An old woman slowly *got off*.

    (Also NS: An old woman slowly *got off* the bus.)

get *on*   **got on**   **[have] got** or **gotten on**   **(I)**

    enter (a large plane or bus or train, or mount a horse) (See also *get into*, above.)

        The old woman had *got on* in Manchester.

    (Also NS: The old woman had *got on* the bus in Manchester.)

get *out*   **got out**   **[have] got** or **gotten out**   **(I)**

    leave (a car or small plane) (often followed by *of*)

        When the car stopped, Tom *got out*.

        He *got out* of the car.

head **into** ____   **headed into**   **[have] headed into**   **(NS**

    drive or fly (a car, plane, etc.) into

        Tom *headed into* the garage.

    (Also S, meaning "move into, turn toward," with two objects: Tom *headed* the car *into* the garage.)

head *out*   **headed out**   **[have] headed out**   **(I)**

    move away from one's present location

        The Jacksons *headed out* toward Springfield.

    (Also S: Tom *headed* the car *out* toward Springfield.)

jack . . . *up* . . .   **jacked up**   **[have] jacked up**   **(S)**

    raise (part of a car, etc.) on a tool called a jack

        To change a tire, one must *jack up* one wheel of the car.

let . . . *down* . . .   **let down**   **[have] let down**   **(S)**

    cause to go down (as the wheels of a plane or as a car on a jack) (See also Chapter 4)

        Let the car *down* slowly with the jack.

pile *out*   **piled out**   **[have] piled out**   **(I)**

    go out of quickly and in a disorderly way (refers to a group, not just one person) (informal)

        The whole family *piled out*.

plow **into** ____   **plowed into**   **[have] plowed into**   **(NS)**

    bump hard against, collide with

        The drunken driver *plowed into* a truck.

pull *in*   **pulled in**   **[have] pulled in**   **(I)**

    arrive, drive, or move into the place to which one is going

        When will the train *pull in*?

pull *over*   **pulled over**   **[have] pulled over**   **(I)**

    drive (a car, etc.) to one side of the road and stop there

        The policeman asked the driver to *pull over*.

    (Also S: The driver *pulled* the truck *over* to the left side.)

put . . . *on* . . .   **put on**   **[have] put on**   **(S)**

    fasten (something) in position (See also Chapter 2)

        Tom and Jim *put* the tire *on*.

run off ____   **ran off**   **[have] run off**   (NS)
 drive (usually unintentionally) off the road, etc., where the vehicle belongs
  Once Tom had to *run off* the road to prevent an accident.

run over ____   **ran over**   **[have] run over**   (NS)
 drive (usually unintentionally) across the top of something
  Most drivers are unhappy if they *run over* an animal.

see . . . *off* . . .   **saw off**   **[have] seen off**   (S)
 watch (someone) go away, go with someone to the place where his or her trip begins
  Good friends sometimes go to an airport to *see* someone *off*.

send . . . *off* . . .   **sent off**   **[have] sent off**   (S)
 say goodbye in a friendly way
  They may *send* the traveler *off* with flowers and other presents.

set *out*   (See Chapter 2)

take *off*   **took off**   **[have] taken off**   (I)
 leave the ground, go into the air (an airplane)
  A plane moves fast along the runway before it *takes off*.

take . . . *off* . . .   **took off**   **[have] taken off**   (S)
 remove
  Fernando has *taken off* the wheel.

turn *around*   **turned around**   **[have] turned around** (I)
 turn to face in the opposite direction, make either a half-circle or a full circle
  When Tom has started on a trip, he does not like to *turn around* and go back.
 (Also S: Tom *turned* the car *around*.)

weave *in* and *out* **weaved in and out** **[have] weaved in and out** (I)
 (When referring to weaving cloth, the past is *wove* and the past participle is *woven*.)
 drive (a car, etc.) quickly past and in front of one vehicle and then another
  Poor drivers *weave in and out* among other cars.

EXERCISES

1. Reading

Read "The Jacksons Set Out on a Trip" several times. If possible, at least one of these readings should be aloud.

2. Answering Questions

Answer each question with a complete sentence. The answers should be those given in the story at the beginning of this chapter. In each answer, use the italicized two-word verb. (It may be necessary to change the form.)

1. Who *got into* their car and *set out*? _____

   _____

2. Who *headed out* toward the highway? _____

   _____

3. What animal *saw* the family *off*? _____

   _____

4. Why did Tom *turn around*? _____

   _____

5. Who *got out* after they *got back* to the house? _____

   _____

6. Did Jane *get in* again? _____

   _____

7. Who *backed out* of the driveway? _____

   _____

8. On her last trip, did Edna *check in* late at the airport? _____

   _____

9. Did she *get on* without waiting long? _____

   _____

10. Did she *get on* the plane without waiting? _____

    _____

11. Who *sent* her *off* with flowers? _____

    _____

12. What did the pilot *let down*? _____

    _____

13. Was there any trouble when the plane *headed into* the unloading area? _____

_____

14. Whom° did Edna see when she *got off* the plane? _____

_____

15. Where did Edna and her parents *dine out*? _____

_____

16. Who *cut in* ahead of the Jacksons? _____

_____

17. Was he *weaving in and out*? _____

_____

18. Did he *run off* the road? _____

_____

19. Did he *run over* some boards and *plow into* a house? _____

_____

20. Why did Tom *pull over*? _____

_____

21. How soon did a policeman *come up*? _____

_____

22. Was Mr. Jackson afraid that their car might *break down*? _____

_____

23. Did the left rear tire *blow out*? _____

_____

24. Who *piled out*? _____

_____

25. Which part of the car did Jim *jack up*? _____

_____

26. Who *took* the tire *off*, and who *put* the spare tire *on*? _____

_____

27. Had Mr. Jackson *figured on* a blowout? _____

_____

28. When did the Jacksons *pull in* at the grandparents' house? _____

_____

° In informal English *who*

INTRANSITIVE VERBS

Intransitive two-word verbs do not take objects. Some verbs, however, such as *back out* and *turn around*, can be either intransitive or separable, as the glossaries show.

In pronouncing intransitive verbs (as well as separable), remember to put a little more stress on the second part than on the main part of the verb: *come **up**, cut **in**, pull **over**, turn **around***.

3. Pronouncing Intransitive Verbs

The following questions and answers use intransitive two-word verbs. Read each aloud. Put a little extra stress on the parts in boldface type.

1. How did Andy *back **out***? He *backed **out*** very carefully.

2. Has a tire ever *blown **out*** while you were driving? Yes, one *blew **out*** last month.

3. What causes most cars to *break **down***? They *break **down*** for many reasons.

4. When did the Jacksons *pull **in***? They *pulled **in*** at four o'clock.

5. When will they *get **back***? They plan on *getting **back*** in three days.

6. Who *got **off*** when the bus stopped? Several sailors have already *got **off***, and others are still *getting **off***.

7. Who *got **out*** when that car stopped? I saw a short woman in a brown coat *get **out***.

8. Does the policeman mean that we should *pull **over***? Yes. I'm *pulling **over*** now.

9. Where is a good place to *turn **around***? George sometimes *turns **around*** at the filling station.

10. Would you like to *set **out*** on a long journey? Yes. I have never *set **out*** for a distant place.

4. Using Intransitive Verbs

Finish each sentence with the most suitable form of the verb in parentheses.

EXAMPLE: (back out) A car is *backing out* _____ of that driveway.
A car was *backing out* _____ of that driveway.
A car *backed out* _____ of that driveway yesterday.
A car has *backed out* _____ of that driveway.

1. (come up) A policeman is _____ now.
A policeman _____ a few minutes ago.
A policeman has _____ .
A policeman may _____ soon.

2. (get back) They will _____ from their trip on Thursday.
They _____ last Thursday.
They have not _____ yet.

3. (blow out) A rear tire _____ while the Jacksons were traveling.
Tires sometimes _____ when they become thin.
Two tires on our truck have _____ today.

4. (take off) The plane is _____ into the wind.
Planes almost always _____ into the wind.

The plane yesterday _____ into the wind.

It has _____ into the wind again today.

5. (set out) The Jacksons will _____ on their trip soon.

They are _____ on their trip now.

They _____ yesterday.

They have _____ on trips before.

ADVERBS WITH TWO-WORD VERBS

Adverbs usually end in *-ly*: *easily, quickly, unexpectedly, usually, suddenly*, etc. Some do not end in *-ly*: *always, soon, often*, etc.

In general, adverbs may be placed with two-word verbs as in these examples:

Intransitive:	The tire SUDDENLY *blew out*.
	The tire *blew out* SUDDENLY.
	SUDDENLY the tire *blew out*.
	(Not: The tire blew suddenly out.)
Separable:	Tom QUICKLY *took* the wheel *off*.
	Tom *took* the wheel *off* QUICKLY.
	QUICKLY Tom *took* the wheel *off*.
	Tom *took off* the wheel QUICKLY.
	Tom QUICKLY *took off* the wheel.
	QUICKLY Tom *took off* the wheel.
	(Not: Tom took quickly off the wheel.)
Nonseparable:	The family SLOWLY *got into* the car.
	The family *got* SLOWLY *into* the car.
	The family *got into* the car SLOWLY.
	SLOWLY the family *got into* the car.
	(Not: The family got into slowly the car.)
Three-Word:	Pedro EASILY *kept up with* Dave.
	Pedro *kept up* EASILY *with* Dave. (Possible but not usual.)
	Pedro *kept up with* Dave EASILY.
	(Not: Pedro kept easily up with Dave. Not: Pedro kept up with easily Dave. Not: Easily Pedro kept up with Dave.)

If all this is difficult to remember, you will usually be right if you put the adverb either before the first word of the verb or at the end of the clause.

5. Using Adverbs with Two-Word Verbs

Say each of the following sentences. Then repeat it, but put the adverb in a different correct place. See the examples under "Intransitive."

1. The family *got in* QUICKLY.

2. A policeman *came up* SOON.

3. We *checked in* LATER at the hotel.

4. The drunken driver RECKLESSLY *cut in*.

5. Tom CAREFULLY *turned around*.

Proceed as in 1−5 above, but give two other placements of the adverb capitalized in each sentence. See the examples under "Separable."

6. The pilot SOON *let* the wheels *down*. (Remember that you can also say *let down the wheels*.)

7. Tom CHEERFULLY *took off* his coat.

8. Jim THEN *put* the spare wheel *on*.

9. Jane SADLY *turned down* the invitation.

10. Edna QUICKLY *cleared* the table *off*.

Again give two other placements. See the examples under "Nonseparable."

11. The driver CARELESSLY *ran over* a pile of sand.

12. One woman *got off* the bus IMMEDIATELY.

13. The rider BOLDLY *headed into* the water.

14. George *rang* SADLY *for* the nurse.

15. Many people OCCASIONALLY *meet with* their lawyers.

This time give only one other placement. See the examples under "Three-Word."

16. George *sat up with* his father FREQUENTLY.

17. The old man HAPPILY *looked back on* his married life.

18. Roy *goes back on* his promise SOMETIMES.

19. Jack AGAIN *got out of* jail.

20. Susan BRAVELY *faced up to* the new problems.

COMMON VERBS WITH "GET"

Over twenty two- and three-word verbs have *get* as the first word.

I. In this chapter:

get back   get off, get off _____   get out
get in   get on, get on _____

II. Before this chapter:

get along (Chapters 1 & 5)   get into _____ (Chapter 2)   get together (Chapter 5)
get away (Chapter 6)   get out of _____ (Chapter 6)   get up (Chapter 2)
get away from _____ (Chapter 1)

III. Here are some other useful verbs with *get*. A common meaning for each one is supplied.

get ahead (I)   move in front (of someone or something), be successful
                                 Helen was the best student in the class for a while, but then Maria
                                  got ahead.
                                  (*Get ahead of* _____ (NS) has the same meaning: Maria *got ahead of* Helen.)

get behind	(I)	go in back of (=*fall behind*, Chapter 1)
		Helen *got behind*.
		(Also NS: Helen *got behind* Maria.)
get by	(I)	manage or succeed in spite of difficult conditions
		There was little food, but we *got by*.
get by _____	(NS)	pass (a car, a runner, etc.) but perhaps with some difficulty
		We finally *got by* the big, slow-moving truck.
get down	(I)	come down (usually to the floor or the ground), descend
		The one-year-old on the chair was afraid to *get down*.
get over _____	(NS)	get well or recover from (an illness or injury)
		Jane *got over* her cold very quickly.
get through	(I)	finish
		George worked until midnight but finally *got through*.
		(Also NS, often followed by *with*: George *got through* [with] his work at midnight.)

6. Using Verbs with "Get"

Which verb from List I fits best in each sentence?

1. Tom opened the car door, _____ , and drove away.

2. Tom opened the car door, _____ , and walked away.

3. Edna went to the airport and _____ the plane for Springfield.

4. She _____ a week later and was glad to be home again.

5. When she _____ the plane, George was there to meet her.

Choose the best verb from List II for each sentence.

6. Tom, Helen, Pedro, and Maria _____ once or twice a week for a meal and some conversation.

7. Sometimes they are tired of schoolwork. They need to _____ it for a while.

8. Good friends usually _____ well together.

9. Sometimes, though, even good friends _____ arguments.

10. Some college students go to bed early and then _____ very early to study.

11. George's father, when he was young, was a robber; but after he _____ jail, he went back to school.

12. Another of the young robbers _____ without being seen and was never caught.

Choose the best verb from List III for each sentence.

13. The Jacksons' cat sometimes races the neighbors' young dog. The dog _____ and tries to keep his lead.

14. But then the cat runs faster and tries to _____ the dog.

76

15. The cat runs still faster, and the dog _____ . He is no longer the leader.

16. When they _____ playing, they lie down near each other and go to sleep.

17. Once the cat climbed a tree and could not _____ .

18. It fell about five meters and was hurt, but it soon _____ its injuries.

7. Making Up an Original Composition

Write several sentences about a real or an imaginary trip that you took in a car or in something else. Use at least ten of the two-word verbs that you have studied in this chapter.

_____

_____

_____

_____

_____

_____

_____

_____

_____

_____

_____

_____

_____

_____

_____

_____

_____

_____

_____

8. Physical Activity

Helen Wears Herself Out

Maria, Helen, Sigrid, and Yuki had been walking and jogging in the woods for most of the afternoon. "I like to *work out* like this," Sigrid said. "It's great to *slip away* from the crowds of students and professors for a while."

Helen was tired. "I wouldn't *feel up to* doing this every day. I've *worn* myself *out*. Are we almost back to our bicycles? I can't *keep up* much longer. I'll *pass out*!" she said jokingly.

"Don't *black out* now," Maria told her. "Of course you could *curl up* in the leaves and sleep. Or you and I could *sit down* for a while and *catch up with* the others later."

"We can *cut across* here," Yuki *pointed out*, "instead of staying on this path. That way will be a little shorter."

"I'll just grit my teeth and *hold on*," said Helen. "I'll *keep up with* you if it kills me. And it probably will! I feel like a fighter who has almost been *knocked out*."

"I'm just *warming up*," Sigrid said. "I could *go on* all night."

"I couldn't," said Yuki. "But I suppose that we should *move on* before it gets dark."

"I'm not *cut out for* this," Helen moaned. "If somebody *asks* us *for* another long run or even walk, I'll say 'No, thanks.' "

"I think that we should *follow up* this jogging with a long walk this evening," said Sigrid. "Walking is easy if you do it right. Just relax and let your body *follow through* each step with your legs and arms moving naturally."

GLOSSARY

INFINITIVE	PAST TENSE	PAST PARTICIPLE	
ask **for** _____	**asked for**	**[have] asked for**	(NS)

request, ask (someone) to give or bring
> The girl *asked for* candy.

(Also S, when there are two objects: The girl *asked* him *for* candy.)

black *out*	**blacked out**	**[have] blacked out**	(I)

faint, become unconscious (=*pass out*)
> Sam *blacked out* and lay on the ground without moving.

catch *up* **with** _____   (See Chapter 1)

curl *up*	**curled up**	**[have] curled up**	(I)

lie down on one's side and pull up one's legs, change from a straight to a curved shape
> "I like to get a good book and *curl up* to read it," she said.

cut **across** _____	**cut across**	**[have] cut across**	(NS)

go straight across or through instead of around
> The distance will be less if we *cut across* the field.

(The object is usually omitted when the meaning is clear without it: "We can save time by *cutting across* here," said Yuki.)

cut *out* **for** _____	**cut out for**	**[have been] cut out for**	(NS)

intended for, made for, suited to, able to do (used only as a passive)
> Some students seem to have been *cut out for* athletics.

feel *up* **to** _____	**felt up to**	**[have] felt up to**	(NS)

feel able to, feel well enough to
> Other students do not *feel up to* walking around the block.

follow . . . *through* . . .	**followed through**	**[have] followed through**	(S)

continue (a movement, plan, etc.) to the end
> A good golfer *follows* the swing *through* so that the club does not stop when it hits the ball.

(Also I: People who play tennis or golf learn to *follow through* when they swing.)

follow . . . *up* . . .	**followed up**	**[have] followed up**	(S)

do (something) next as a continuation of
> Sigrid *followed up* her walk with a swim in the pool.
> A good salesman *follows up* each lead that he receives.

go *on*	**went on**	**[have] gone on**	(I)

continue
> The path they were following went on through the woods.

(Also NS, often followed by an *-ing* word: He *went on* talking.)

hold *on*	**held on**	**[have] held on**	(I)

continue to try
> Helen *held on* and finally got home.

keep *up*, **keep** *up* **with** _____   (See Chapter 1)

knock . . . *out* . . .   **knocked out**   [have] **knocked out**   (I)
    make weak and helpless, make unconscious (perhaps by hitting)
        The short boxer *knocked out* his taller opponent.

move *on*   **moved on**   [have] **moved on**   (I)
    go forward again
        The students reached the edge of the woods and then *moved on*.

pass *out*   **passed out**   [have] **passed out**   (I)
    faint, become unconscious (=*black out*) (informal)
        Of course, Helen did not really *pass out*.

point . . . *out* . . .   **pointed out**   [have] **pointed out**   (S)
    call attention to, show
        Yuki *pointed out* a shorter way home.

sit *down*   (See Chapter 3)

slip a*way*   **slipped away**   [have] **slipped away**   (I)
    go away quietly, go without being seen
        "Often I like to *slip away* and be alone," Sigrid said.

warm *up*   **warmed up**   [have] **warmed up**   (I)
    practice or exercise for a few minutes before a contest, performance, etc.;
    become accustomed to doing something (See also Chapter 4)
        Almost all singers *warm up* before a performance.

wear . . . *out* . . .   **wore out**   [have] **worn out**   (S)
    cause to become very tired   (See also Chapter 4)
        The long walk *wore* Helen *out*.
    (Also I, become very tired: I *wear out* too quickly.)

work *out*   **worked out**   [have] **worked out**   (I)
    do physical exercise, run or lift weights, etc., to exercise the body
        Many students *work out* frequently in the gymnasium.
    (Also S: Horse trainers *work* their horses *out* each day.)

EXERCISES

1. Reading

Read "Helen Wears Herself Out" several times. Be ready to read any part of it aloud.

2. Substituting

What two-word or three-word verb (from this lesson) could be used instead of the italicized part of each sentence? The first letter of the word is in parentheses. In a complete sentence, write the form that is needed.

1. "I like to *do physical exercise* in this way," Sigrid said.   (w) _____

   _____

2. I enjoy *going away quietly* from the crowds.   (s) _____

   _____

3. Helen said, "I wouldn't *feel able to* do this every day."   (f) (Change *do* to *doing*.) _____

   _____

4. I have *caused* myself *to become very tired*.   (w) _____

   _____

5. I cannot *stay even* much longer.   (k) _____

   _____

6. "I'll *faint*!" she said jokingly.   (p) _____

   _____

7. "Don't *become unconscious* now," Maria said.   (b) _____

   _____

8. You could *lie down* in the leaves *and pull up your legs* and sleep.   (c) _____

   _____

9. Or you and I could *change to a sitting position* for a while.   (s) _____

   _____

10. We could *overtake* the others later.   (c) _____

    _____

11. Yuki *called attention to* something.   (p) _____

    _____

12. We could *go straight across*.   (c) _____

    _____

13. "I'll just grit my teeth and *continue to try*," Helen said.   (h) _____

_____

14. "I'm just *practicing*," Sigrid said.   (w) _____

_____

15. I could *continue* all night.   (g) _____

_____

16. Yuki said, "I suppose that we should *go forward again*."   (m) _____

_____

17. "I'm not *suited to* this," Helen moaned.   (c) _____

_____

18. If somebody *requests* another long walk or run, I'll say "No, thanks."   (a) _____

_____

19. "I think we should *do something as a continuation of* this," Sigrid asserted.   (f) _____

_____

20. Walking is easy if you let your body *continue* each step *to the end*.   (f) _____

_____

NEGATIVES

Negatives of Two-Word Verbs
After these helping verbs + *not*:

be (am, is, are, was, were, been)

Generally use this form:

-ING OR PAST PARTICIPLE
Sigrid was not ***sitting*** down.
The girls were not really ***worn*** out.

do (does, did)
may (might)
can (could)
shall (should)
will (would)
must
ought to

SIMPLE FORM
Helen did not ***keep*** up.
She could not ***go*** on.
She will not ***pass*** out.

have (has, had)

PAST PARTICIPLE
Tom has not ***warmed*** up
Ella has not ***sat*** down.

Note 1: *Be* or *been* is also sometimes used with a verb from the second or third group, in sentences like these:

Helen may not be following through.
Maria has not been sitting down.
Tom may not have been sitting down.

Note 2: In informal speech and writing, *not* is often shortened to *n't* in these words:

isn't, aren't, wasn't, weren't
mayn't (rare), mightn't
shan't (rare; =shall not), shouldn't
mustn't

don't, doesn't, didn't
can't, couldn't
won't (=will not), wouldn't
haven't, hasn't, hadn't

3. Using Negatives

Make each of the following sentences negative in four different ways. Use each verb in parentheses with *not* or *n't*. Sometimes you will need to change the form of the two-word verb.

EXAMPLE: (did, will, am, have)   I asked for new shoes.

I did not ask for new shoes.
I won't ask for new shoes.
I am not asking for new shoes.
I have not asked for new shoes.

1. (does, will, may, must)   Helen slips away from the others.

_____

_____

_____

_____

2. (can, should, did, ought to)   Helen and Maria catch up with their friends. (Put *not* between *ought* and *to*.) _____

_____

_____

_____

3. (did, has, should, might)   Helen curled up in the leaves.

_____

_____

_____

_____

4. (is, does, must, may)   Tom follows through when he swings his tennis racket.

_____

_____

_____

_____

5. (did, will, has, ought to)   Dave pointed out Tom's mistake.

_____

_____

_____

_____

6. (does, had, is, must)   Maria sits down. _____

_____

_____

_____

7. (do, have, are, may)   They go on. _____

_____

_____

_____

8. (did, must, should, would) They cut across a farmer's pasture.

_____

_____

_____

_____

9. (does, was, has, should) Sigrid works out daily. _____

_____

_____

_____

10. (did, has, may, will) Helen felt up to walking a long distance.

_____

_____

_____

_____

IMPERATIVES

An imperative sentence commands or requests someone to do something. When *please* is used, it makes the command or request more polite.

EXAMPLES: Move on. Please move on. Move on, please.
Point out the right answer. Please point out the right answer.
Point it out. Please point it out. Point it out, please.
Don't sit down. Please do not sit down. Will you sit down. Will you please sit down.

Notice that the last examples look like questions but are really requests. That is why periods are used instead of question marks.

4. Using Imperatives

Change each group of mixed-up words and punctuation marks into an imperative sentence. Do not leave out or add any words.

1. down sit . _____

2. down please . sit _____

3. down sit . please , _____

4. car into . get the _____

5. into please . get the car _____

6. into , please . get the car _____

7. you will up , please . stand _____

8. you will up please . stand _____

9. grass the . don't across cut _____

10. don't please . the across grass cut _____

11. away early , please slip . _____

12. hat off your . take _____

13. it . off take please _____

14. it , off . take please _____

15. you your . will take hat please off _____

5. Making Up Original Sentences

Write several sentences telling about taking a long walk. Use at least seven of the two- or three-word verbs that you have studied in this chapter.

_____

_____

_____

_____

_____

_____

_____

_____

_____

_____

_____

_____

_____

_____

_____

_____

_____

_____

_____

_____

9. Business (I)

The Jacksons Set Up Their Own Business

George Jackson liked to repair small engines. He could take an old lawnmower, for instance, and *fix* it *up* so that it ran like a new one. He and his wife often *talked over* the possibility of *setting up* their own business of selling and repairing small engines.

"When I was young, I always **planned** *on* having my own business," he reminded her one night when the twins were away. "If I could *do* it *over*, I would *go into* business much earlier. Edna, this may be the best time. We have *paid off* all our debts and *saved up* a little money. Starting a new business is risky, but my job at the factory is not safe either. The company *laid off* thirty of its newest workers last week because its sales have *slackened off*. Mr. Green **sent** *for* me today and told me that orders have *dropped off* so much that the company may have to *lay* me *off*, too."

"That's awful, George," Edna said. "But do you believe we could *work up* enough business in our own shop to pay our expenses? I could *give up* my part-time job and *help out* with the selling and the accounts. I'd finally be able to use my bookkeeping and accounting skills again."

"*Building up* a business is often slow," he said. "Many businesses just *inch along* for several years. But I think that if we try hard we'll make enough money that we can *live on* it. You could sell the new engines and the parts and the tools, and I could *tune up* the old engines that need to be repaired. I believe that things would *work out* well enough."

"Where would we *set up* shop?"

"We could *take over* that empty building on Main Street. I talked with the owner today, and he wanted me to *sign up* at once. I told him I wanted to *talk* it *over* with you. He may *hold out for* more rent than I am willing to pay, but I believe we can *work out* an agreement unless we become *bogged down* in some of the details. What do you think we should do, Edna?"

"I think we should **sleep** *on* it."

GLOSSARY

INFINITIVE	PAST TENSE	PAST PARTICIPLE	
bog . . . *down* . . .	**bogged down**	**[have] bogged down**	(S)

be slowed, be hindered, become stuck
> The plans for the shop were *bogged down* for a while.

(Also I: The plans *bogged down*.)

build . . . *up* . . .	**built up**	**[have] built up**	(S)

make strong or large or successful, create slowly, develop, cause to increase
> Henry Ford *built up* a very large business.

(Also I, increase slowly: His anger *built up* during the day.)

do . . . *over* . . .	**did over**	**[have] done over**	(S)

do again, repeat (an action or a series of actions), repeat in a better way
> When people make mistakes, they often must *do* their work *over*.

drop *off*	**dropped off**	**[have] dropped off**	(I)

become less, be reduced (prices, sales, etc.)
> Profits *dropped off* in the winter.

fix . . . *up* . . .	**fixed up**	**[have] fixed up**	(S)

repair, put into working order, improve the appearance of
> George had often *fixed up* his own mower.

give . . . *up* . . .	(See Chapter 2)		

***go* into ____**	**went into**	**[have] gone into**	(NS)

enter, begin, start (a business, an activity, or a condition)
> Can one *go into* business with very little money?

help *out*	**helped out**	**[have] helped out**	(I)

assist, provide help
> Many young people *help out* in their parents' shops.

(Also S: His wife *helps* him *out*.)

hold *out* for ____	**held out for**	**[have] held out for**	(NS)

insist on getting before coming to an agreement
> Did the owner *hold out for* too much money?

inch *along*	**inched along**	**[have] inched along**	(I)

move very slowly, move a small distance at a time
> The street was icy, so cars could only *inch along*.

(Also NS: Cars *inched along* the icy street.)

lay . . . *off* . . .	**laid off**	**[have] laid off**	(S)

drop (someone) from employment for a while
> The factory has *laid off* a hundred workers.

***live* on ____**	**lived on**	**[have] lived on**	(NS)

exist on; have enough food, etc., to survive on
> How much money does this family need to *live on*?

pay . . . *off* . . .	**paid off**	**[have] paid off**	(S)

pay all that one owes
> Some families never *pay* their debts *off*.

plan on ____   planned on   [have] planned on   (NS)
    make plans or preparations for (usually followed by an *-ing* word)
        The Jacksons were *planning on* buying some small engines to sell to others.

save . . . *up* . . .   **saved up**   **[have] saved up**   (S)
    save a small amount at a time
        The Jacksons had *saved up* a few thousand dollars.
    (Also I: They had to *save up* for years.)

send for ____   **sent for**   **[have] sent for**   (NS)
    ask (someone) to come or bring
        George's employer *sent for* him.
        We *sent for* some medicine.

set . . . *up* . . .   **set up**   **[have] set up**   (S)
    start, establish (*set up shop* = start a small business)
        Can the Jacksons *set up* a business that will be successful?

sign *up*   **signed up**   **[have] signed up**   (S)
    write one's name on a paper agreeing to do something
        One should not *sign up* without thinking carefully about it.

slacken *off*   **slackened off**   **[have] slackened off**   (I)
    become less (as sales, business, profits, etc.), become slower (*Slack off* is also used.)
        Often a business *slackens off* during part of the year.

sleep on ____   slept on   [have] slept on   (NS)
    delay or postpone (a decision) until the next morning (often in the phrase *sleep on it*)
        "Let's not decide now. Let's *sleep on it*," Edna said.

take . . . *over* . . .   **took over**   **[have] taken over**   (S)
    become responsible for, take charge of, become the owner of
        Sometimes a new owner *takes over* an old business.

talk . . . *over* . . .   (See Chapter 4)

tune . . . *up* . . .   **tuned up**   **[have] tuned up**   (S)
    adjust properly, cause to operate smoothly and correctly (usually a machine or a
    musical instrument)
        An automobile engine should be *tuned up* after a few thousand kilometers.

work *out*   **worked out**   **[have] worked out**   (I)
    proceed satisfactorily, be or become acceptable or successful (See also Chapter 8)
        Will the Jacksons' plans *work out*?

work . . . *out* . . .   **worked out**   **[have] worked out**   (S)
    develop with someone else (an arrangement, etc.), make adjustments in a plan, etc.
        The Jacksons need to *work out* many details with other people.

work . . . *up* . . .   **worked up**   **[have] worked up**   (S)
    develop (a plan, a business, etc.) (often = *build up* or *work out*)
        They *worked up* a budget for the year.

EXERCISES

1. Reading

Read "The Jacksons Set Up Their Own Business" several times. Be ready to read any part of it aloud.

2. Answering Questions

Answer each question with a complete sentence. Use the correct form of the two- or three-word verb in parentheses. Reread parts of "The Jacksons Set Up Their Own Business" if you need to.

1. What could George Jackson do to an old lawnmower? (fix . . . up . . .) _____

2. What did George and Edna talk over? (talk . . . over . . . , set . . . up . . .) _____

3. What plans did George make when he was young? (plan . . . on . . .) _____

4. If he could start over, what would he do? (go into ___) _____

5. What have the Jacksons done to their debts? (pay . . . off . . .) _____

6. Have they saved any money? (save . . . up . . .) _____

7. What did the company do to thirty workers? (lay . . . off . . .) _____

8. Why did the company do that? (slacken off) _____

9. What did Mr. Green do? (send for ___) _____

10. What had happened to the company's orders? (drop off) _____

11. What did Edna promise to do if they started a business? (help out) _____

12. Is building up a business often easy? (build . . . up . . .) _____

13. How fast do many businesses grow?   (inch along) _____

_____

14. Does George believe that the Jacksons can exist on their income from the new business?

(live on ____) _____

_____

15. What will George do to old engines?   (tune . . . up . . .) _____

_____

16. What could the Jacksons do to the empty building?   (take . . . over . . .) _____

_____

17. Did the owner want George to sign an agreement?   (sign up) _____

_____

18. What did George tell him?   (talk . . . over . . .) _____

_____

19. What did George think the owner might do?   (hold out for ____) _____

_____

20. Did George believe that an agreement might be reached?   (work . . . out . . .) _____

_____

21. What did Edna think they should do?   (sleep on ____) _____

_____

3.   Using Verbs in Other Contexts

The following sentences use some of the same verbs as those in Exercise 2, but they are not about the Jacksons. Choose the verb that better fits the meaning of the sentence.

1. When sales _____ very much, a factory may need to close.   (drop off, take over)

2. More often, however, the factory _____ some of its workers.   (fixes up, lays off)

3. The workers' families then must _____ smaller amounts of money and food. (go into, live on)

4. Some families _____ money for use at a future time.   (save up, sign up)

5. _____ one's own business requires a great deal of planning.   (Setting up, Tuning up)

6. It is not wise to make an important decision without thinking carefully. A person should at least _____ it.   (hold out for, sleep on)

7. It may take years to _____ a good business.   (build up, slacken off)

8. Not all of a person's plans _____ .   (take over, work out)

9. In a small business, all members of the family may need to _____ . (bog down, help out)

10. When a person makes a mistake, he or she must often _____ the work _____ . (do over, take over)

11. When one has a serious problem, it may be necessary to _____ an expert for help. (send for, work up)

12. The owner of a small business often hopes to _____ all of his or her debts. (lay off, pay off)

13. In almost every business, sales _____ during some parts of the year. (set up, slacken off)

14. An owner likes to have someone else who can _____ the responsibility in case of illness. (work up, take over)

15. Most business people _____ making changes from year to year. (go into, plan on)

LONG OBJECTS WITH SEPARABLE VERBS

In the sentences below, the complete objects are in capital letters.

Clear:	I could *tune up* THE OLD ENGINES THAT NEED TO BE REPAIRED.
Confusing, awkward:	I could *tune* THE OLD ENGINES THAT NEED TO BE REPAIRED *up*.
Clear:	The company *laid off* ABOUT THIRTY OF ITS NEWEST WORKERS last week.
Slightly confusing, awkward:	The company *laid* ABOUT THIRTY OF ITS NEWEST WORKERS *off* last week.

When the object of a separable verb is several words long, it should usually not be placed between the parts of the verb.

4.   Using Long Objects with Separable Verbs

Put each object where it seems most clear. Short objects, as you know, may usually be put either between the parts of the separable verb or at the end. Pronouns like *it* and *them*, of course, must separate the parts.

OBJECTS

1.
George could fix up

- old engines
- them
- an engine that no one else could repair

_____

_____

_____

2.

George and Edna talked over
{
it
the possibility of starting a new business
one possibility
}

_____

_____

_____

3.

The Jacksons have paid off
{
all the debts that they once owed
them
their debts
}

_____

_____

_____

4.

Do you believe we could build up
{
enough business
enough business to succeed
it
}

_____

_____

_____

5.

We could take over
{
it
that building
that empty building on Main Street
}

_____

_____

_____

6.

We could work out
{
agreements satisfactory to all of us
them
satisfactory agreements
}

_____

_____

_____

7.

The clown took off $\left\{\begin{array}{l}\text{them} \\ \text{five shirts} \\ \text{all the shirts that he had on}\end{array}\right.$

_____

_____

_____

8.

The clown put on $\left\{\begin{array}{l}\text{it} \\ \text{a colorful hat} \\ \text{a red, green, and yellow straw hat}\end{array}\right.$

_____

_____

_____

9.

Robbers held up $\left\{\begin{array}{l}\text{the bank at the corner of Sixth and Main} \\ \text{a bank} \\ \text{it}\end{array}\right.$

_____

_____

_____

10.

Edna picked out $\left\{\begin{array}{l}\text{them} \\ \text{two tomatoes} \\ \text{the two largest tomatoes that she could find}\end{array}\right.$

_____

_____

_____

5. Trying Variations

Read each of the following sentences. Then change it in the ways suggested.

EXAMPLE: The Jacksons *set up* their own business.

(Did) *Did the Jacksons set up their own business?*

(are) *The Jacksons are setting up their own business.*

(did not) *The Jacksons did not set up their own business.*

1.   George and Edna *talked* the matter *over.*

(Did) _____

(are) _____

(may not) _____

2. The Jacksons *pay off* all their debts.

(are) _____

(have) _____

(cannot) _____

3. The company is *laying off* thirty workers.

(may) _____

(has) _____

(Is the) _____

4. Mr. Green *sends for* Mr. Jackson.

(sent) _____

(Did) _____

(Why did) _____

5. The Jacksons may *take over* an old building.

(not) _____

(have) _____

(Will) _____

6. George *meets with* the owner.

(Has) _____

(will) _____

(yesterday.) _____

7. The owner is *holding out for* more rent.

(was) _____

(may) _____

(has) _____

8. The Jacksons *sleep on* their decision.

(are) _____

(have) _____

(last night.) _____

9. George *tunes up* many small engines.

(Will) _____

(last month.) _____

(is) _____

10. The Jacksons *keep on* trying.

(will) _____

(Will) _____

(have) _____

6. Making Up Original Sentences

Turn back to this chapter's glossary. Close your eyes and put your finger on one of the two-word verbs. Make up an original sentence in which you use it. Repeat for at least nine other verbs.

_____

_____

_____

_____

_____

_____

_____

_____

_____

_____

_____

_____

_____

_____

_____

_____

_____

_____

10. Business (II)

Everybody Helps Out

After *sleeping on* the problem, the Jacksons decided to *set up* their own business. They and the owner of the Main Street building *agreed on* the amount of rent and *settled on* other details. After they had signed an agreement, George told Edna, "Well, it can't be *called off* now."

"No," she said, "we can't *back out of* the deal now. But I'll hate to *part with* all that rent money every month."

"I think that everything will *turn out* all right," he said hopefully. "Just as long as we don't *run out of* money. But we have *lived through* difficult times before."

"If we just do not lose money this year," she said, "we'll be doing all right. I suppose that we can't *count on* more than that."

They *shopped around*, trying to find the best kinds of machines to sell. They also tried to find the best companies to *deal with*. They *checked up on* the reputation of each company. One dealer, they *found out*, seemed to be *making off with* money that was not his own. So his offer was *turned down* at once. Finally they *singled out* a company that seemed honest and that sold good machines. "We want to *deal with* only the companies that *live up to* their agreements," the Jacksons said.

Forms were *filled in*. Money was *paid down* on everything they bought. Prices were *going up* constantly. The money that had been *laid aside* was disappearing too fast. Some bonds that they had hoped to keep were being *cashed in*.

The twins *helped out* in cleaning and painting the building. They knew that their father was no longer *putting in* time at the factory and that the family had to *live off* the money from the little shop. They tried to be cheerful. "*Cheer up*, Dad," Jane said one day. "We'll *stick to* this business until it *pays off*."

"We'll never *sell out* or *shut* the business *down*," Tom wrote from college. "I'll *pitch in* during the summer and do as much as I can."

GLOSSARY

agree *on* ____   **agreed on**   **[have] agreed on**   (NS)
    consent to, accept (an agreement or the terms of a business deal) (= *settle on*)
        The Jacksons and the owner *agreed on* other things besides the rent.

back *out* **of** ____   **backed out of**   **[have] backed out of**   (NS)
    change one's mind about, break a promise about, withdraw from
    (See also *go back on*, Chapter 6)
        Sometimes it seems necessary to *back out of* an agreement.

call . . . *off* . . .   **called off**   **[have] called off**   (S)
    cancel, stop, bring an end to
        Should the Jacksons have *called off* the signing of the agreement?

cash . . . *in* . . .   **cashed in**   **[have] cashed in**   (S)
    get cash instead of, sell (usually bonds or stocks), redeem
        When the Jacksons *cashed in* their bonds, they received several thousand dollars.

check *up* **on** ____   **checked up on**   **[have] checked up on**   (NS)
    examine to discover the facts about
        Please *check up on* the truth of this story.

cheer *up*   **cheered up**   **[have] cheered up**   (I)
    become cheerful, become happy and pleasant
        Jane hoped that her father would *cheer up*.
    (Also S, make cheerful: Jane *cheered* her father *up*.)

count **on** ____   **counted on**   **[have] counted on**   (NS)
    depend on, rely on, expect, be sure of
        Can one *count on* the honesty of all companies?

deal **with** ____   **dealt** [dĕlt] **with**   **[have] dealt** [dĕlt] **with**   (NS)
    do business with, buy from or sell to
        Do you like to *deal with* business people who are not honest?

fill . . . *in* . . .   **filled in**   **[have] filled in**   (S)
    write in (blanks, etc.), complete by writing in
        Have all the blanks been *filled in*?

find . . . *out* . . .   (See Chapter 1)

go *up*   **went up**   **[have] gone up**   (I)
    increase (prices), become higher
        Prices of food have *gone up* again.

help *out*   (See Chapter 9)

lay . . . *aside* . . .   **laid aside**   **[have] laid aside**   (S)
    keep for later use, save, put away (*Put* . . . *aside* . . . has the same meaning.)
        Has any money been *laid aside*?

live **off** ____   **lived off**   **[have] lived off**   (NS)
    exist on what is earned from, exist on available funds or land
    (See also *live on* ____ , Chapter 9)
        The Jacksons had to *live off* the income from the shop.

live through _____	lived through	[have] lived through	(NS)

exist in spite of (something difficult or unpleasant)
> Many people *live through* weeks when they are hungry.

live *up* to _____	lived up to	[have] lived up to	(NS)

do (whatever is promised), act according to
> George found out that many business people do *live up to* their agreements.

make *off* with _____	made off with	[have] made off with	(NS)

steal, take, go away with (something that is probably not one's own)
> Some workers *make off with* their employers' tools.

part with _____   (See Chapter 4)

pay . . . *down* . . .	paid down	[have] paid down	(S)

pay part of the cost of when one buys
> On a two hundred dollar machine, George *paid down* fifty dollars and owed one hundred and fifty.

pay *off*	paid off	[have] paid off	(I)

produce a profit
> Will the Jacksons' business *pay off*?

(Also S, with a different meaning. See Chapter 9)

pitch *in*	pitched in	[have] pitched in	(I)

help, assist, provide help (informal) (= *help out*)
> Everyone must *pitch in* if a small business is to succeed.

put . . . *in* . . .	put in	[have] put in	(S)

spend, use (time) (See also Chapter 1)
> Some people like to *put in* their spare time in painting.

run *out* of _____	ran out of	[have] run out of	(NS)

use all of, have no more
> "There's nothing left to eat," she said. "We've *run out of* food."

sell *out*	sold out	[have] sold out	(I)

sell, sell all of
> Some business people must *sell out* during the first year.

(Also S: The Jacksons *sold out* their lawnmowers.)

settle on _____	settled on	[have] settled on	(NS)

consent to, accept, decide on (the arrangement or the terms of a business deal) (= *agree on*)
> The Jacksons *settled on* the terms for buying their machines.

shop *around*	shopped around	[have] shopped around	(I)

examine several possibilities before buying something
> George likes to *shop around* to find the best machines.

shut . . . *down* . . .	shut down	[have] shut down	(S)

close, stop operating (a business or a factory)
> When a business is *shut down*, it no longer buys, manufactures, or sells.

(Also I: Some businesses *shut down* and then reopen.)

single . . . *out* . . .   **singled out**   **[have] singled out**   (S)
       select, choose (usually just one)
           The Jacksons *singled out* one company to supply most of their chain saws.

***sleep* on ____**   (See Chapter 9)

***stick* to ____**   **stuck to**   **[have] stuck to**   (NS)
       persist in, continue doing
           "I won't give up," George said. "I'll *stick to* this business."

turn . . . *down* . . .   **turned down**   **[have] turned down**   (S)
       refuse (See also Chapter 5)
           He *turned down* some offers that seemed unreasonable.

turn *out*   **turned out**   **[have] turned out**   (I)
       end, result, get (good or bad) results, eventuate
           How will the Jacksons' business efforts *turn out*?

EXERCISES

1. Reading

Read "Everybody Helps Out" several times. Be ready to read any part of it aloud.

2. Choosing the Right Word

Select the verb from each group that fits best in each sentence. Look back at the story if necessary.

   turn out   called off   agreed on   back out of   part with

1. The Jacksons and the owner _____ the rent.

2. George said, "The deal can't be _____ now."

3. Edna said, "We can't _____ it now."

4. They hated to _____ so much money each month.

5. "Maybe everything will _____ all right," George said.

   shopped around   dealt with   count on   lived through   run out of

6. I hope we don't _____ money.

7. We have _____ trouble before.

8. We can't _____ making much money the first year.

9. The Jacksons _____ to find the machines they could sell at a profit.

10. They finally _____ several companies.

   making off with   turned down   checked up on   singled out   found out

11. They _____ the reputation of each company.

12. They _____ that some companies were more honest than others.

13. One dealer seemed to be _____ other people's money.

14. The Jacksons _____ his offer.

15. They _____ one especially good company.

   paid down   lived up to   went up   filled in   laid aside

16. They wanted companies that _____ their agreements.

17. They _____ many forms.

18. They _____ money _____ on everything they bought.

19. Prices _____ constantly.

20. The Jacksons had _____ some money which they now had to spend.

live off   cheer up   cashed in   helped out

21. They _____ some of their bonds.

22. The twins _____ in the evenings and on weekends.

23. The family had to _____ the income from the small business.

24. Jane told her father to _____ .

pitch in   stick to   pay off   shut down   sell out

25. "We'll _____ this business," Jane said.

26. Someday it will _____ .

27. "We'll never _____ ," Tom wrote.

28. We will not _____ the business _____ .

29. I'll _____ during the summer.

3.   Reading Aloud

Read aloud the sentences you completed for Exercise 2.

PASSIVE VERBS

	SUBJECT	ACTIVE VERB
Active:	The Jacksons	turned down the offer.

	SUBJECT	PASSIVE VERB
Passive:	The offer	was turned down.

In a sentence in the active voice, the subject *acts*; it does something. The Jacksons acted by turning down the offer.

In a sentence in the passive voice, the subject does not act; it does not do anything. In the second sentence above, the offer does not act.

The passive voice of a verb usually consists of a form of *be* and the past participle of the verb.

Singular

The offer
{
is
was
may be, can be, will be, etc.
has been, should have been, etc.
}
turned down.

Plural

The offers
{
are
were
may be, can be, will be, etc.
have been, may have been, etc.
}
turned down.

Intransitive verbs cannot be passive.

Sometimes a phrase with *by* is added after a passive verb to tell who or what performs the action.

The offer was *turned down* by the Jacksons.

4. Using Passive Verbs

Change each of these sentences to make it passive. Start with the word or words that have been supplied.

EXAMPLES: They agreed on the price. The price *was agreed on*.

Ahmed and Ali agreed on a price. (Use *by*.) The price *was agreed on by Ahmed and Ali.*

A detective checked up on Ali's story. (Use *by*) Ali's story *was checked up on by a detective.*

1. The Jacksons and the owner agreed on the amount of rent. The amount _____

   _____

2. They settled on other details. Other _____

   _____

3. We cannot count on large profits. Large _____

   _____

4. We cannot call it off now. It _____

   _____

5. One dealer made off with a large amount of money. (Use *by*.) A large _____

   _____

6. The Jacksons singled out one reliable company. (Use *by*.) One _____

   _____

7. They would deal with only the honest companies. Only _____

   _____

8. They fill in many forms. Many _____

   _____

9. They pay down some money on each purchase. Some _____

   _____

10. They had laid aside some money. (Use *had been*.) Some _____

    _____

11. They had cashed in some bonds. Some _____

    _____

12. We will never sell out the business. The _____

    _____

13. We will never shut the business down. The _____

    _____

14. The Jacksons have taken over the building on Main Street. (Use *has been* and *by*.) The building _____

    _____

15. They have set up their business there. Their _____

    _____

16. Mr. Jackson tuned up nine engines in one day. (Use *by*.) Nine _____

    _____

17. They have picked out the engines that they will sell. The _____

    _____

18. The new business has brought about many changes in their lives. (Use *by*.) Many _____

    _____

19. They have put off a planned trip to Europe. A _____

    _____

20. They have worn out much of their clothing. Much _____

    _____

TWO-WORD VERBS WITH "TURN"

Usually a verb with *turn* suggests movement of some kind. Several such verbs are presented in this book.

In this chapter:

turn . . . down . . . (See also Chapter 5)
turn out

In earlier chapters:

turn around (Chapter 7)   turn . . . off . . . (Chapter 2)
turn in (Chapter 4)   turn . . . on . . . (Chapter 2)
turn . . . in . . . (Chapter 1)

Others:

turn against _____ (NS)   stop helping, take support away from, become an enemy of
                              Some people *turn against* their friends.

turn into _____ (NS)   become (something very different), be changed to
                              In an old story, a frog *turned into* a prince.
                              (Also S, with two objects: A pretty girl *turned* a frog *into*
                              a prince.)

turn . . . **over** . . . (S)   look at from several angles (in one's mind), think about in various
                              ways, consider
                              The Jacksons *turned* the problem *over* in their minds and
                              then made a decision.

turn up (I)   be found unexpectedly, come unexpectedly

> Uncle John Jackson, who had not been there for years, *turned up* last Tuesday.

5. Using Two-Word Verbs with "Turn"

Which of the verbs listed above fits best in each of these sentences?

1. Jim walked from his house to the shop, _____ , and came back home.

2. One of George's old shoes was missing, but it _____ in the neighbors' yard.

3. Another factory offered George a job, but he _____ it _____ .

4. Tom _____ his paper _____ to the teacher on the day it was due.

5. Mr. Jackson was sleepy. "I think I'll _____ ," he said.

6. When the Jacksons need to make an important decision, they usually _____ the matter _____ in their minds for a while.

7. Jim wanted to see a football game, so he _____ the television _____ .

8. Jane did not like football, so she _____ it _____ .

9. The Jacksons are having problems with their business, but they hope that everything will _____ well.

10. George said, "In the past, one businessman sometimes helped another but then _____ him after a disagreement."

11. Edna was hopeful, "Some small businesses," she reminded the family, "have _____ large companies."

12. The Jacksons will probably not _____ their small business _____ a large one.

6. Making Up Original Sentences

Write an original sentence for each of these verbs:

agree on ____	fill . . . in . . .	sell . . . out . . .
call . . . off . . .	lay . . . aside . . .	shut . . . down . . .
cash . . . in . . .	pay . . . down . . .	single . . . out . . .
count on ____	pay . . . off . . .	turn . . . down . . .
deal with ____		

_____

_____

_____

_____

_____

_____

_____

Change into a passive form each of the sentences that you wrote above.

11. Business (III)

Totaling Up the Profits and Losses

Edna Jackson *disposed of* several small engines each week, and George usually **worked on** thirty or forty mowers, chain saws, garden tractors, and the like. Bst even though they *took in* considerable money, they also had to *pay out* a great deal. Their income was small, and the family as a result often had to *do without* things that they wanted.

When they *settled up* their bills at the end of each month, they *figured out* that their income usually *amounted to* somewhat more than their expenses. From the total income they had to *take off* part for taxes. They had *put up* a lighted sign, which cost several hundred dollars. They also advertised by *handing out* free pencils to people who *came into* the shop, and of course those were an additional expense. Edna sometimes *counted out* a few dollars to help the poor or the sick as contributions to charity.

George had to *send away for* machine parts every week. If they sold a machine for three hundred dollars, their own costs usually *added up to* at least two hundred and fifty.

Sometimes they *sold off* some of their machines at lower prices. They would need to *close out* machines that were no longer being made, so they would *mark* the prices *down*. Sometimes, of course, the Jacksons could *mark* prices *up*. Sometimes, too, they could *buy out* another dealer's merchandise or *buy up* part of his machines. In those ways they *kept* their own costs *down*. They had not known that so many shops *dealt in* small engines.

At the end of their first year, George and Edna and their children *totaled up* their profits and losses. They had about thirty machines that they could *carry over* to the next year. But some people had not paid what they owed, and the family knew that they would have to *write off* some of those accounts as bad debts.

When they had finished, George *summed up* the year. "Well, we *took in* enough money to **live on**, but we'll probably never get rich. Anyhow, we will not need to *give up* the business because we have at least made a living. We can *carry on with* it next year, and maybe the profits will be better then. Let's *send out for* some fried chicken to celebrate."

GLOSSARY

INFINITIVE	PAST TENSE	PAST PARTICIPLE	
add *up* to ____	**added up to**	**[have] added up to**	(NS)

total, equal (= *amount to*)
> The Jacksons' expenses *added up to* a large sum.

amount to ____	**amounted to**	**[have] amounted to**	(NS)

total, equal (= *add up to*)
> The Jacksons' expenses *amounted to* a large sum.

buy...*out*...	**bought out**	**[have] bought out**	(S)

purchase all of
> The Jacksons *bought out* the engines of one dealer who had died.

buy...*up*...	**bought up**	**[have] bought up**	(S)

buy, purchase all that one can of
> They *bought up* most of another dealer's tools.

carry *on* with ____	**carried on with**	**[have] carried on with**	(NS)

continue, keep doing
> The Jacksons were happy because they could *carry on with* the shop.

(*Carry on* is also S: They *carried on* the business for another year. Also I: They *carried on* for another year.)

carry...*over*...	**carried over**	**[have] carried over**	(S)

(as a business term) hold or keep for future sale
> Business people always *carry over* some merchandise from one year to the next.

close...*out*...	**closed out**	**[have] closed out**	(S)

sell all of (usually at a lower price)
> Many clothing stores *close out* summer clothing in August.

***come* into ____**	**came into**	**[have] come into**	(NS)

enter (Note that *come into* is used with an object. *Come in* has the same meaning but takes no object.)
> On some days few buyers *came into* the shop.

count...*out*...	**counted out**	**[have] counted out**	(S)

count one by one
> The little girl carefully *counted out* seven pennies.

***deal* in ____**	**dealt [dĕlt] in**	**[have] dealt [dĕlt] in**	(NS)

buy and sell (certain kinds of things)
> That small shop *deals* only *in* decorated flower pots.

dis*pose* of ____	**disposed of**	**[have] disposed of**	(NS)

sell, give away, or trade; get rid of
> First a store buys something, and then it tries to *dispose of* it.

do without ____   (See Chapter 3)

figure . . . out . . .   (See Chapter 1)

give . . . up . . .   (See Chapter 2)

hand...*out*...   **handed out**   **[have] handed out**   (S)
    give one by one, hand to others one by one
        In some food stores, clerks *hand out* small samples of cheese or a new product.

keep...*down*...   **kept down**   **[have] kept down**   (S)
    hold as low as possible (costs or prices)
        The Jacksons tried to *keep* their costs *down*.

live **on** ____   (See Chapter 9)

mark...*down*...   **marked down**   **[have] marked down**   (S)
    reduce or lower (prices), change a price tag to show a lower price
        Edna *marked* the price *down* from $85.00 to $69.95.

mark...*up*...   **marked up**   **[have] marked up**   (S)
    increase or raise (prices), change a price tag to show a higher price
        Then she *marked* another price *up* from $150.00 to $169.50.

pay...*out*...   **paid out**   **[have] paid out**   (S)
    spend, expend, pay (an amount of money)
        The Jacksons *paid out* several hundred dollars for insurance.

put...*up*...   **put up**   **[have] put up**   (S)
    build, construct, erect
        Perhaps sometime the Jacksons will *put up* their own building.

sell...*off*...   **sold off**   **[have] sold off**   (S)
    sell, sell all of, dispose of
        A few farmers *sold off* their cattle because feed was so expensive.

send *away* **for** ____   **sent away for**   **[have] sent away for**   (NS)
    order from a (usually) distant place
        Many people still *send away for* their clothing and other things.

send *out* **for** ____   **sent out for**   **[have] sent out for**   (NS)
    call or send a message asking someone to bring (something)
        College students sometimes *send out for* sandwiches and coffee.
    (Also S, with two objects: George *sent* Jim *out for* fried chicken.)

settle...*up*...   **settled up**   **[have] settled up**   (S)
    pay (an amount that one owes); pay off everything owed
        Many people *settle up* their bills on the first of each month.

sum...*up*...   **summed up**   **[have] summed up**   (S)
    summarize, say briefly, say or write in a few words
        George *summed up* the events of the past year.

take...*in*...   **took in**   **[have] taken in**   (S)
    receive (money, etc.), get, obtain, secure (said especially of a store or other business)
        Perhaps the Jacksons will *take in* more money next year.

take...*off*...   **took off**   **[have] taken off**   (S)
    deduct, subtract from
        The Jacksons *took off* a few dollars from the price.

total . . . ***up*** . . .   **totaled** [or **totalled**] **up**   [**have**] **totaled** [or **totalled**] **up**   (S)
   add up, find the total of
      When tax-paying time comes, people must first *total up* their income.

work **on** ____   **worked on**   [**have**] **worked on**   (NS)
   repair, try to correct something broken, spend time on
      Some people like machines and enjoy *working on* them.

write . . . ***off*** . . .   **wrote off**   [**have**] **written off**   (S)
   cancel, accept as a loss
      One man could not pay the Jacksons the fifty dollars he owed them, and
      they *wrote* it *off* as a bad debt.

EXERCISES

1. Reading

Read "Totaling Up the Profits and Losses" several times. Be ready to read any part of it aloud.

2. Choosing the Right Verb

Select the verb at the left that fits best in each sentence.

paid out   took in   did without   disposed of   worked on

1. Edna was a good salesperson. In some weeks she _____ several small engines.

2. Mowers often need to be repaired. Some days George _____ several of them.

3. From selling and repairing, the Jacksons _____ considerable money.

4. They also _____ a great deal of money because their expenses were high.

5. Since the family did not have much money, they often _____ things that they wanted.

putting up   take off   settle up   amount to   hand out

6. Business people always hope that their income will _____ more than their expenses.

7. Some people each month try to _____ whatever they owe.

8. _____ a lighted sign can be expensive.

9. Very few business people now _____ gifts to their customers.

10. "Last month," said George, "we had to _____ from our income several hundred dollars for taxes."

sent away for   close out   added up to   mark up   count out

11. Little children in a candy store _____ their nickels and dimes very carefully.

12. When George needed some parts for a mower, he _____ them.

13. Total costs for one garden tractor _____ eleven hundred dollars.

14. When George and Edna want to stop selling one kind of mower, they _____ the ones they have.

15. When their own costs go up, shopkeepers _____ the price tags for their customers.

marked down   buy out   bought out   dealt in   sold off

16. The Jacksons wished that they could _____ someone else's machines at a low price.

17. Once a dealer in another town was going out of business. The Jacksons _____ all his garden tractors.

18. They _____ those tractors to their customers at lower prices.

19. That is, they _____ the price tags on those tractors.

20. The Jacksons' small-engine shop was not the only one in town. Several others also _____ small engines.

   sum up   lived on   send out for   carry on with   totaled up

21. At the end of the year the Jacksons sat down and _____ their profits and losses.

22. George tried to _____ the results of the year.

23. "At least we have _____ the income from the store this year," he said.

24. We can _____ the business again next year.

25. To celebrate, let's _____ some fried chicken.

TWO- AND THREE-WORD VERBS

Sometimes a word like *in, on, of, for,* or *with* can be added to an intransitive two-word verb. The whole three-word group then takes an object.*

INTRANSITIVE TWO-WORD VERB	TRANSITIVE THREE-WORD VERB	MEANING OF THE TRANSITIVE VERB	EXAMPLES
back out	**back out of**	break a promise about	He *backed out of* the agreement.
break in	**break in on**	interrupt	He *broke in on* the conversation.
burst in	**burst in on**	enter without knocking, etc.; interrupt	She *burst in on* the meeting.
carry on	**carry on with**	continue	She *carried on with* her work.
catch on	**catch on to**	understand	He *caught on to* the rules quickly.
catch up	**catch up with**	overtake	Tom *caught up with* Helen.
check out	**check out of**	pay one's bill when leaving	We *checked out of* the hotel.
come along	**come along with**	accompany, come with	She *came along with* her sister.
drop in	**drop in on**	visit, visit without previous arrangement	We *dropped in on* the Joneses.
drop out	**drop out of**	quit, stop doing or going to	He *dropped out of* school.
fill in	**fill in for**	replace, substitute for	Mr. Adams *filled in for* our teacher that day.

---

* Sometimes it is difficult to say whether a sentence has a three-word verb or a two-word verb followed by a prepositional phrase. The three-word groups listed here, however, work together as a unit and usually have the meaning of a single verb.

INTRANSITIVE TWO-WORD VERB	TRANSITIVE THREE-WORD VERB	MEANING OF THE TRANSITIVE VERB	EXAMPLES
get ahead	get ahead of	pass, move in front of	The other runner *got ahead of* me.
go on	go on with	continue	Please *go on with* your work.
hold on	hold on to	grasp, keep one's hands around or on	The baby *held on to* her mother's dress.
keep on	keep on with	continue	She *kept on with* her reading.
keep up	keep up with	go as fast as, match or equal (someone else in speed, etc.)	I ran fast, but she *kept up with* me.
look out	look out for	be careful about, be watchful for, avoid (= *watch out for*)	*Look out for* slippery places on the road.
run away	run away from	leave, run to avoid or escape	Please don't *run away from* me.
take up	take up with	befriend, become a friend of	He *takes up with* strange people.
talk back	talk back to	answer in an impolite way	She *talked back to* her father.
think back	think back on	remember, recall	The old woman *thought back on* her girlhood.
warm up	warm up to	become friendly or favorable toward	Most people quickly *warm up to* Fred.
watch out	watch out for	be careful about (= *look out for*)	*Watch out for* the dog.

3. Using Two- and Three-Word Verbs

Make up a short original sentence with each of the three-word verbs in the list above. If you wish, you may make only small changes in the examples that are given.

_____

_____

_____

_____

_____

_____

_____

_____

_____

_____

_____

_____

_____

_____

_____

_____

_____

_____

_____

_____

_____

TWO-WORD VERBS WITH "TAKE"

Verbs with _take_ are often related in meaning to _get_ or _carry_.
Review the definitions of any of these verbs that you have forgotten:

take . . . in . . .   (Chapter 11)   take . . . out . . .   (Chapter 5)
take off   (Chapter 7)   take . . . over . . .   (Chapter 9)
take . . . off . . .   (Chapters 7 & 11)   take . . . up . . .   (Chapter 4)
take . . . on . . .   (see Chapter 12)

4.   Using Two-Word Verbs with "Take"

Which of those seven verbs fits best in each sentence?

1.   The plane went fast down the runway and then _____ .

2.   George got his tools and _____ the top of the mower.

3.   I'll _____ you _____ in a race, Dave.

4.   How much money did the shop _____ last week?

5.   The meeting was long. It _____ more than two hours of our time.

6.   Sometimes one person may _____ another person's business.

7.   Tom told Dave that he would _____ Helen _____ Saturday evening.

TWO-WORD VERBS WITH "PUT"

Verbs with *put* are usually related in meaning to *place*.
Look up the definitions of any of these verbs that you do not know:

put . . . aside . . . (Chapter 10)	put . . . off . . . (Chapter 1)
put . . . away . . . (Chapter 2)	put . . . on . . . (Chapters 2 & 7)
put . . . down . . . (see Chapter 13)	put . . . up . . . (Chapter 11)
put (heads) together (see Chapter 15)	put up with ____ (Chapter 5)
put . . . in . . . (Chapters 4 & 10)	

5.   Using Two-Word Verbs with "Put"

Which of those nine verbs fits best in each sentence?

1.   The Jacksons had _____ a few thousand dollars to use in the future.

2.   The twins finally learned to _____ their clothing in the clothes closet.

3.   The family often _____ their heads _____ before making a decision.

4.   Many students _____ their studying until very late.

5.   Some friends of the Jacksons are _____ a new house. They hope to move in next summer.

6.   Jane _____ a green dress this morning.

7.   Edna kept the business records of the shop. She _____ in a book all the income and all the expenses.

8.   Business people must _____ high costs and high taxes.

9.   When the twins were talking about school, Jim _____ some remarks about Spanish class.

TWO-WORD VERBS WITH "KEEP"

Verbs with *keep* are usually related in meaning to *hold* or *continue*.
Review the definitions of any of these verbs that you have forgotten:

keep at ____ (Chapter 1)	keep up (Chapter 8)
keep . . . down . . . (Chapter 11)	keep . . . up . . . (Chapter 4)
keep on ____ (Chapter 2)	keep up with ____ (Chapter 11)
keep on with ____ (Chapter 11)	

6.   Using Two-Word Verbs with "Keep"

Which of those seven verbs fits best in each sentence?

1.   Jim ran so fast that Tom could not _____ .

2.   She could not _____ him.

3.   George _____ working hard.

4.   In busy times, George _____ his work even after dark.

5. Most business people try to _____ their expenses _____ .

6. "Work hard," George told his children. "If something is difficult to do, just _____ it."

7. All the Jackson children _____ their schoolwork.

7. Making Up Original Sentences

Choose from this chapter's glossary the verbs that you are not sure you know well. Write an original sentence with each.

_____

_____

_____

_____

_____

_____

_____

_____

_____

_____

_____

_____

_____

_____

_____

_____

_____

_____

12. Competition

Pushing On to Victory

Tom and Dave often ran races against each other, in practice for track meets with other teams. The coach tried not to **side** *with* either runner, but he *cheered* **on** both boys in their races against other schools. The boys were good friends, but both liked to *show off* their athletic ability. One evening they were talking and joking with their coach about their latest practice race.

"It was an exciting race," Tom said. "I *got behind* at first."

"That's when I should have *speeded up*," Dave said. "But I made the mistake of *slowing down* too much to save my breath. I *let up* too soon."

"Yes, so I *caught up*. But you *hung on*. Then I *pulled* a little *ahead*, and I *came through* gloriously at the end."

"*Came through* gloriously!" Dave exclaimed. "You just barely *beat* me *out*!"

"I was *faced with* defeat, but I *made up* about ten meters and *pushed on* to a splendid victory."

"Splendid victory! I bravely *fought* you *off* until the end, and then you *nosed* me *out*. I'll *carry off* the splendid victory next time!"

"No, I'm too fast for you now," Tom said. "I think that I can *shut* you *out* in all our races after this."

Dave *laughed off* Tom's boast. He said to the coach, "You know he can't do that. Aren't you going to *stand* **up** *for* me?"

"I'll never **turn** *against* you, Dave," the coach told him. "I always *back* **up** all members of the team. I always **root** *for* all of you."

"Coach, you're just trying not to *stir* **up** trouble. That's why you're not choosing sides," Dave said with a grin.

"No, I'm only saying that I won't *hold* it **against** you if you do lose to another member of our team. But you'd still better *speed* **up** so you can *take* **on** the runners from the other teams next Saturday."

GLOSSARY

back . . . *up* . . .   **backed up**   **[have] backed up**   (S)
support, help, be loyal to (= *stand up for*)
    Will you *back* me *up* in the argument?

beat . . . *out* . . .   **beat out**   **[have] beaten out**   (S)
win against (in competition), defeat in a close contest (informal)
    Taller athletes do not always *beat out* shorter ones.

carry . . . *off* . . .   **carried off**   **[have] carried off**   (S)
win (a prize, a victory, an honor, etc.)
    Who *carried off* the prize in the 1500-meter run?

catch *up*   **caught up**   **[have] caught up**   (I)
become even with, come up to someone else in a competition
(See also *catch up with*, Chapter 1)
    The Los Angeles team is still trying to *catch up*.

cheer . . . *on* . . .   **cheered on**   **[have] cheered on**   (S)
support by cheering (yelling, shouting, clapping, etc.)
    Their friends are *cheering* them *on*.

come *through*   **came through**   **[have] come through**   (I)
be successful, win, last successfully to the end
    Did your favorite team *come through*?

***face* . . . with . . .**   **faced with**   **[have] faced with**   (S)
meet, encounter (especially something difficult or unpleasant) (generally
used as a passive: [be] *faced with*)
    Has she ever been *faced with* serious problems?
(Active: The police *faced* him *with* new evidence.)

fight . . . *off* . . .   **fought off**   **[have] fought off**   (S)
keep (someone or something) away or behind, fight successfully against
(an enemy of any sort), repel
    The leader *fought off* the runner in second place.

get be*hind*   **got behind**   **[have] got or gotten behind**   (I)
let (someone else) move in front, fail to get or hold the leading position
(=*fall behind*, Chapter 1)
    Often a team *gets behind* but then catches up.

hang *on*   **hung on**   **[have] hung on**   (I)
continue to try hard
    The leader *hung on* and finally won.

hold . . . *against* . . .   **held against**   **[have] held against**   (S)
object to, be unhappy about, be displeased with (often in the phrase
hold it against [someone])
    Would Dave *hold* it *against* Tom if he forgot his birthday?

laugh . . . *off* . . .   **laughed off**   **[have] laughed off**   (S)
fail to consider seriously, dismiss by laughing
    Was Helen angry? No, she just *laughed* it *off*.

let *up*   **let up**   **[have] let up**   (I)

try less hard, go more slowly
> Sometimes the leader in a contest *lets up* too soon.
> The rain *let up*.

make . . . *up* . . .   **made up**   **[have] made up**   (S)

gain (in competition), reduce a difference (in distance or time)
> Dave led by several meters, but Tom soon *made* that distance *up*.

nose . . . *out* . . .   **nosed out**   **[have] nosed out**   (S)

defeat in a close contest, defeat by a small distance, amount, total, etc.
> Jack *nosed out* Andy in the election, 1,172 to 1,146.

pull a*head*   **pulled ahead**   **[have] pulled ahead**   (I)

move in front, take the lead
> When did Tom finally *pull ahead*?

push *on*   **pushed on**   **[have] pushed on**   (I)

make a continuing effort, continue in difficult conditions
> A good athlete *pushes on* even when he knows he will probably lose.

***root* for ____**   **rooted for**   **[have] rooted for**   (NS)

support by cheering, etc. (informal) (=*cheer on*)
> Their friends are *rooting for* them.

show . . . *off* . . .   (See Chapter 5)

shut . . . *out* . . .   **shut out**   **[have] shut out**   (S)

keep someone from scoring at all (in contests)
> Cleveland *shut out* New York by a score of 6−0.

***side* with ____**   **sided with**   **[have] sided with**   (NS)

agree with, support
> If both Smith and Jones want to become the President, which one will
> you *side with*?

slow *down*   **slowed down**   **[have] slowed down**   (I)

go more slowly than before (=*slow up*)
> In automobile races, some drivers almost never *slow down*.

speed *up*   **sped** or **speeded up**   **[have] sped** or **speeded up**   (I)

go faster than before
> They are getting closer to us. Can't you *speed up*?

(Also S, cause to go faster: He *speeded up* the engine.)

stand *up* for ____   **stood up for**   **[have] stood up for**   (NS)

support, talk in favor of (=*back up*)
> "*Stand up for* what you believe," George told Tom.

stir . . . *up* . . .   **stirred up**   **[have] stirred up**   (S)

start, cause, put into motion
> "Don't *stir up* trouble if you can avoid it," he also said.

take . . . *on* . . .   **took on**   **[have] taken on**   (S)

start to compete against, challenge (in a contest)
> Detroit will *take on* San Diego in another game.

INFINITIVE	PAST TENSE	PAST PARTICIPLE	
turn against ____	**turned against**	**[have] turned against**	(NS)

stop helping, take one's support away from, stop being in favor of, become hostile or unfriendly toward

      Some of the players *turned against* their manager.

EXERCISES

1. Reading

Read "Pushing On to Victory" several times. If possible, read it aloud in groups of four. One person may be the narrator, and the other three may read what Tom, Dave, and the coach say.

2. Substituting

What two-word verb studied in this chapter has about the same meaning as the italicized part of each sentence? The first letter has been given. Rewrite the sentence using the form that is correct.

1. Dave's friends usually *supported* him *by shouting and clapping*. (c) _____

   _____

2. Many boys and some girls like to *make a display of* their athletic ability. (s) _____

   _____

3. When Tom and Dave were racing, Tom *let* Dave *move in front* in the first hundred meters. (g)

   _____

4. Later Tom *went faster than before* and came closer. (s) _____

   _____

5. Then he *became even* and moved ahead. (c) _____

   _____

6. Dave had *run more slowly than before*. (s) _____

   _____

7. He had *tried less hard*. (l) _____

   _____

8. In life, as in a race, it is important to *continue to try hard*. (h) _____

   _____

9. In their race, Tom *lasted successfully to the end*. (c) _____

   _____

10. Tom finally *won against* Dave. (b) _____

    _____

11. At one time Tom was *encountering* defeat. (f) _____

    _____

12. Early in the race Tom was ten meters behind Dave. He was able to *gain* that distance. (m) _____

    _____

13. Try to *make a continuing effort* even if you lose. (p) _____

_____

14. In a close race the leader must try to *keep* the other runners *behind*. (f) _____

_____

15. A winner sometimes only *defeats* an opponent *by a small distance*. (n) _____

_____

16. Tom said that Dave could never win another race from him—that he could *keep* Dave *from winning at all*. (s) _____

_____

17. Dave *did not consider seriously* Tom's boast. (l) _____

_____

18. Dave hoped the crowd would *support* the team in the next contest. (st) _____

_____

19. Loyal supporters never *take their support away from* a team even when it loses. (t) _____

_____

20. Students at State University generally *are loyal to* their team. (b) _____

_____

21. Athletes like to have the crowd *support* them *by cheering*. (r) _____

_____

22. Some people seem to enjoy *causing* trouble. (s) _____

_____

23. Should you *be displeased with* people because they do not agree with you? (h) (Add *it*.) _____

_____

24. The State University runners will *start to compete* against other teams next week. (t) _____

_____

25. Perhaps Dave can *go faster* and win his next race. (s) _____

_____

NOUNS FROM TWO-WORD VERBS

Some two-word verbs have come to be used as nouns also. The simple form of the verb is the one used in each of these nouns. See the examples below.

3. Pronouncing

In pronouncing the noun, stress the first part slightly.
Read these pairs of sentences.

TWO-WORD VERB	NOUN BASED ON THE VERB
1. Two front tires *blow out*.	*Blowouts* can be dangerous.
2. The machinery may *break down*.	There was a *breakdown* in the machinery.
3. Someone might *break in* if we leave.	We had a *break-in* at our house.
4. The ruler should *build up* the army.	The *buildup* of the army was slow.
5. The Jacksons will *carry over* some debts to the next year.	The *carry-over* will be small.
6. The people *cry out* against high taxes.	There was a loud *outcry*. (In this word, note that *out* comes before *cry*.)
7. Sales will *drop off*.	There will be a *drop-off* in sales.
8. A good golfer *follows through* on his swing.	That golfer's *follow-through* is weak.
9. They and their friends often *get together*.	They had a *get-together* with their friends.
10. Sam may *knock* the other fighter *out*.	Sam won by a *knockout*.
11. The factory will *lay off* thirty workers.	The *layoff* may get larger.
12. Dave *let up* when he was ahead.	There should have been no *letup*.
13. Suspected criminals had to *line up*.	The *lineup* was a short one.
14. We must *look out* for the approach of the enemy.	A *lookout* watched for the approach of the enemy.
15. Edna had to *mark down* (*up*) some prices.	The *markdowns* (*markups*) were small.
16. Don't *mix up* the price tags.	A *mix-up* could be serious.
17. The rich man had to *pay off* the blackmailer.	The *payoff* was large.
18. Edna tried to *sell out* all the mowers.	It was her first *sellout*.
19. The factory *shut down*.	The *shutdown* may last more than a month.
20. The baseball team *shut out* its opponents, 4 to 0.	There are often *shutouts* in baseball.
21. The driver needed to *speed up*.	The *speedup* was sudden.
22. Good friends *stand by* one another.	You are my old *standby*.
23. The plane will soon *take off*.	The *takeoff* was smooth.
24. George *tunes up* engines.	This engine needs a *tuneup*.
25. Tom and Dave *work out* daily.	They enjoy their *workouts*.
26. Jim will *write up* his lesson.	His *write-up* is two pages long.

4. Using Nouns Based on Two-Word Verbs

Choose ten of the italicized nouns in the second column above. Make up an original sentence with each.

_____

_____

_____

_____

_____

_____

_____

_____

_____

_____

5. Forming Questions

Change each of the following statements into a question that uses the same two-word verb. (Change the form of the verb if necessary.) The first word or words of your question have been given.

EXAMPLE: Tom *nosed out* Dave in the race in Green Park.

Where *did Tom nose out Dave?* _____

1. We should *back up* our team. Should _____

_____

2. Tom *beat out* Dave in a race yesterday. When _____

_____

3. Tom *caught up* with Dave in the last fifty meters. Who _____

_____

4. Tom *carried off* the victory. Who _____

_____

5. Their friends *cheered* the runners *on* because they liked both boys. Why _____

_____

6. I try to *come through* with a victory. Do you usually _____

_____

7. Everyone is *faced with* difficulties in making good decisions. Is _____

_____

8. It is necessary for everyone to *fight off* troubles. Who must _____

_____

9. All of us sometimes *get behind*.   Is it true that _____

_____

10. We should not *hold* it *against* Dave if he loses again.   Should _____

_____

11. Most people can *laugh off* defeat.   Can _____

_____

12. Often a person loses because he or she *lets up* too soon.   What happens if _____

_____

13. In the race Tom was ten meters behind, but he *made up* that distance.   How much distance _____

_____

14. A race horse named Rascal *nosed out* Double Trouble and Old Harry.   Which horse _____

_____

15. During the first month of the baseball season, the Giants *pulled far ahead*.   When _____

_____

16. The swimmers *pushed on* even when the waves began to get high.   Did _____

_____

17. Students will still *root for* the team.   Will _____

_____

18. Tom *showed off* his speed.   Who _____

_____

19. Helen usually *sided with* Tom.   Who° did Helen _____

_____

20. Both teams *shut out* their opponents.   Did _____

_____

21. Drivers usually *slow down* on slick roads.   Do _____

_____

22. The driver of a white car was *speeding up* and getting away.   Who _____

_____

23. My father always *stood up for* what he believed was right.   What did my _____

_____

_____
°*Whom* in formal English.

24. Edna *stirred up* some new problems when she talked about taxes. <u>When</u> _____

_____

25. Pedro and Fernando *took on* Tom and Dave in a swimming contest. <u>Who° did Pedro and</u>

<u>Fernando</u> _____

26. Most parents do not *turn against* a child who loses. <u>Do</u> _____

_____

6. Making Up Original Sentences

Turn to this chapter's glossary. If your first name has an odd number of letters (1, 3, 5, etc.), write an original sentence using the first, third, fifth, and so on of the verbs listed—fourteen sentences in all. If your first name has an even number of letters (2, 4, 6, etc.), write an original sentence with the second, fourth, and so on—thirteen sentences in all.

_____

_____

_____

_____

_____

_____

_____

_____

_____

_____

_____

_____

_____

_____

_____

_____

° *Whom* in formal English.

13. Reading and Writing

Jane and Jim Go About Writing an Assignment

Jim and Jane were *talking over* an assignment for their English class.

"As I understand it," Jane said, "each of us must *write up* the most important points that *came up* in the class discussion of the book."

"Yes, but I don't know how to *go about* it. Should we *go into* everything that was said? Or should we just *bring out* the details of two or three points? Just what is the teacher *driving at*?"

"I don't know, Jim. In class I *put down* almost everything that anyone said. And, of course, I *looked up* some other information. But the teacher wouldn't want us to *write* everything *out* in too much detail."

"I should *look up* what I wrote in my notes, too. Then I can *thumb through* them and *pick out* the most important parts."

"I may *stumble across* a couple of things that are especially interesting and important. Then maybe I can just *sum up* the others, while *dwelling on* only those two."

"That sounds good, Jane. As I understand the assignment, we don't need to *write down* much about the book itself. We shouldn't tell what *became of* each person or even how the story *came out*."

"Right. I really enjoyed the story. I don't know how an author can *make up* something so exciting. It's really simple, but he *spun* it *out* by including many vivid details. I want to *read up on* the author and *find out* more about him."

"I think that he has written a new book, Jane. Did you know that the library *subscribes to* several magazines that print book reviews?"

"Yes, I've *dipped into* some of them."

"Well, I'll *draw up* a plan for my paper now, and decide which two or three points I should *play up*."

"So will I. I'm sure that our papers will *turn out* all right."

GLOSSARY

INFINITIVE	PAST TENSE	PAST PARTICIPLE	
be*come* of ____	**became of**	**[have] become of**	(NS)

happen to

    What *became of* the girl at the end of the story?

bring . . . *out* . . .	**brought out**	**[have] brought out**	(S)

write, tell, include, present, produce, reveal

    Good writers *bring out* useful information about people.

come *out*	**came out**	**[have] come out**	(I)

end (of a story or a happening in a person's life), end up (=*turn out*)

    How did your talk with the teacher *come out*?

come *up*	**came up**	**[have] come up**	(I)

be mentioned, be discussed, occur, happen (See also Chapters 4 and 7)

    Several surprising things *came up* in class that day.

***dip* into** ____	**dipped into**	**[have] dipped into**	(NS)

look at (a book, magazine, theory, etc.) very quickly

    I won't read all of it. I'll just *dip into* it.

draw . . . *up* . . .	**drew up**	**[have] drawn up**	(S)

make (a plan, outline, etc.); prepare

    Before writing, a person should usually *draw up* a plan.

***drive* at** ____	**drove at**	**[have] driven at**	(NS)

intend, mean, try to do or find out (*Driving at* is the usual form.)

    When you asked me about Cynthia, what were you *driving at*?

***dwell* on** ____	**dwelled on** or **dwelt on**	**[have] dwelled on** or **dwelt on**	(NS)

emphasize, pay much or most attention to; think, write, or speak about for a long time, concentrate on

    Some authors *dwell on* the sadness of life, others on its pleasures.

find . . . *out* . . .   (See Chapter 1)

***go* about** ____	**went about**	**[have] gone about**	(NS)

start, proceed with

    How should I *go about* writing a story?

***go* into** ____	**went into**	**[have] gone into**	(NS)

discuss, consider (in writing or speaking)

    The author *went into* the history of the building of the first transcontinental railroad.

look . . . *up* . . .   (See Chapter 1)

make . . . *up* . . .	**made up**	**[have] made up**	(S)

create, invent (a story, sentence, etc.) (See also Chapters 1 and 12)

    Making up a story is easy for some writers.

pick . . . *out* . . .   (See Chapter 3)

play . . . *up* . . .	**played up**	**[have] played up**	(S)

pay most attention to, emphasize

    Jane *played up* the class's comments on two people in the story.

put . . . *down* . . .   **put down**   **[have] put down**   (S)

write, take notes on, make a written record of

Jim had *put down* some information that Jane thought was not important.

read *up* **on** _____   **read up on**   **[have] read up on**   (NS)

read information about, read to become well-informed about

I'd like to *read up on* the early railroads.

spin . . . *out* . . .   **spun out**   **[have] spun out**   (S)

make long, extend, add many details to (a story or other writing)

Some authors *spin out* a story too much, and it becomes boring.

stumble **across** _____   **stumbled across**   **[have] stumbled across**   (NS)

happen to find (=*run across*, Chapter 5. *Stumble on* or *onto* or *into* and *happen on*
have the same meaning.)

One can *stumble across* some strange facts while reading.

sub*scribe* **to** _____   **subscribed to**   **[have] subscribed to**   (NS)

pay money in order to receive regularly (usually a magazine or a newspaper)

Does your family *subscribe to* any magazines?

sum . . . *up* . . .   (See Chapter 11)

talk . . . *over* . . .   (See Chapter 4)

thumb **through** _____   **thumbed through**   **[have] thumbed through**   (NS)

turn pages quickly while glancing at the contents

I like to *thumb through* a book to find out whether I would enjoy it.

turn *out*   (See Chapter 10)

write . . . *down* . . .   **wrote down**   **[have] written down**   (S)

put into writing

We cannot *write down* everything that a speaker says.

write . . . *out* . . .   **wrote out**   **[have] written out**   (S)

write all of, put numbers or abbreviations into full written form

Write out this number instead of using figures.

write . . . *up* . . .   **wrote up**   **[have] written up**   (S)

write an account or a description of, write in detail, write from notes

In science class, Jim has to *write up* what happened in an experiment.

EXERCISES

1. Reading

Read "Jane and Jim Go About Writing an Assignment" several times. Be ready to read it aloud with a partner. One person should read Jane's speeches, and the other should read Jim's.

2. Substituting

In the following sentences synonyms have been used for the two-word verbs. What two-word verb could be used instead of the italicized part? The first letter of the verb is in parentheses. Write out the new sentence.

1. Jane and Jim *discuss* their English assignment.   (t) _____
_____

2. "Each of us needs to *write from our notes* the most important points," Jane said.   (w) _____
_____

3. I mean the points that *were mentioned* in class discussions of the book.   (c) _____
_____

4. "I don't know how to *proceed with* it," said Jim.   (g) _____
_____

5. Should we *consider* all that everyone said?   (g) _____
_____

6. Or should we just *include* the details on two or three points?   (b) _____
_____

7. What is the teacher *intending*?   (d) _____
_____

8. Well, I *took notes on* all that was said.   (p) _____
_____

9. Also, I *searched for and found* some other information.   (l) _____
_____

10. But the teacher certainly doesn't want us to *write all* that was said.   (w   o) _____
_____

11. "I'll *turn the pages rapidly and glance at* my notes," said Jim.   (t) _____
_____

12. Then I can *select* the best parts.   (p) _____
_____

13. "I thought I might *happen to find* a couple of very interesting things," Jane said. (s) _____

_____

3. Substituting

Continue as in Exercise 2.

1. Then I'll just *summarize* the others. (s) _____

_____

2. I'll say that I will *pay most attention to* only two points. (d) _____

_____

3. Good. We don't need to *put into writing* much about the book itself. (w) _____

_____

4. For example, we shouldn't tell what *happened to* the main character. (b) _____

_____

5. We shouldn't tell how the story *ended*, either. (c) _____

_____

6. "I don't know how an author can *create* such an exciting story," Jane commented. (m) _____

_____

7. He *made* the story *long* by including so many interesting details. (s) _____

_____

8. I want to *read information about* the author. (r) _____

_____

9. I hope to *discover* more about him. (f) _____

_____

10. Jane, do you know that the library *pays money to receive* several magazines that print book reviews? (s) _____

11. Yes. I've *looked quickly at* some of them. (d) _____

_____

12. I'll *prepare* a plan for my paper now. (d) _____

_____

13. I'll decide which two or three points I should *emphasize*. (p) _____

_____

14. So will I. I believe that our papers will *end* all right. (t) _____

_____

4. Using Other Tenses

Each of the following sentences is in the present tense. Change each verb in three ways. First write the past tense. Then write the form with the past participle, including *have* or *has*. Finally, write the form needed after the word in the third blank.

EXAMPLE: What <u>becomes of</u> (*became of* , *has become of* , may *become of*) last year's best-selling books?

1. Jane *brings out* (_____ , _____ ,

    may _____) points that are different from Jim's.

2. The story *comes out* (_____ , _____ ,

    should _____) with a happy ending.

3. Several interesting points *come up* (_____ , _____ ,

    might _____) in class.

4. The author *dwells on* (_____ , _____ ,

    did _____) one character.

5. Jim and Jane *find out* (_____ , _____ ,

    must _____) how to write a good summary.

6. Jim *draws up* (_____ , _____ ,

    can _____) a very clear plan for his paper.

7. The twins *go into* (_____ , _____ ,

    do not _____) all the points discussed in class.

8. The author *makes up* (_____ , _____ ,

    may _____) an unusual story.

9. Jane *puts down* (_____ , _____ ,

    should _____) the most important points.

10. Jim *reads up on* (_____ , _____ ,

    will _____) the author's life.

11. The author *spins out* (_____ , _____ ,

    could _____) the story in exciting detail.

12. Jim *sums up* (_____ , _____ ,

    will _____) the results.

13. Each twin *writes down* (_____ , _____ ,

    should _____) only what is important.

14. Jane *writes out* (_____ , _____ ,

    will _____) her paper in ink.

15. Jane and Jim *write up* (_____ , _____ ,

    must _____) a summary of class discussion.

5. Making Up Original Sentences

From this chapter's glossary choose all the verbs that you do not know very well. Make up an original sentence with each.

_____

_____

_____

_____

_____

_____

_____

_____

_____

_____

_____

_____

_____

_____

_____

_____

_____

_____

14. Speaking

Speaking About Speaking

"The English language is tricky," Maria said to Helen one day. "I still have trouble with some of the little words. Tell me the differences between *speak of*, *speak about*, and *speak for*."

"Your English is excellent," Helen said, "but maybe I can answer a few questions. If we mention something, we **speak** *of* it or **speak** *about* it. They mean the same thing. But if we *speak* *for* something, we speak in favor of it. Right now we're **speaking** *of* language or **speaking** *about* it, but we're not *speaking* *for* anything."

"What about some of the verbs with *talk*?"

"Let me think. Well, if we *talk* **back** *to* a person, we say something in answer to what he or she said or did, and back talk is sometimes not very respectful or polite. If we *talk* **down** *to* a person, we treat her or him as inferior to us, less intelligent or more childish than we are. But if we *talk* **up** a plan or even a party, we are talking in favor of it, and—"

"What if I interrupt someone, as I did just now?"

"You could say that you *broke* **in**, even though you didn't really 'break.' *Butt* **in** is an informal way to say the same thing. You could also say that you *broke* **in** on what I was saying."

"I can think of some others. Are these right? If we end a conversation, we *break* it **off**. If something hurts or excites me, I may *cry* **out**, which seems to mean about the same as 'exclaim' or 'yell.' If I say something very suddenly—maybe something I shouldn't—I *blurt* it **out**. Are those right?"

"Yes. And if a crowd of people yell to keep you from talking, they *shout* you **down**. They may do that because you are *speaking* **out** by expressing your opinion frankly."

"Last night I read a conversation in a book, in which the author said that one of the characters *chimed* **in**. What does that mean?"

"It means that the person was adding something to what was just said, probably agreeing with it. If people disagree with somebody's plan, they may try to *talk* the person **out** *of* doing it."

"We've **touched** *on* some of the verbs I wanted to **speak** *about*, but I'm sure there will be more. Oh, I just **thought** *of* another. I heard a little girl say to her brother, 'Don't **tell** *on* me.' What did she mean?"

"Probably she had done something she shouldn't have done, and she was asking her brother not to tell her parents. We could *talk* **on and on** about expressions like these."

"Yes, I suppose we could *go* **on and on**."

GLOSSARY

blurt . . . *out* . . .   **blurted out**   [**have**] **blurted out**   (S)
   say something very suddenly and perhaps without thinking
     "That's not true!" I *blurted out.*

break . . . *in* . . .   **broke in**   [**have**] **broken in**   (S)
   interrupt, speak before someone else has finished
     "Did he—" "Look at that dog!" she *broke in.*

break *in* on ____   **broke in on**   [**have**] **broken in on**   (NS)
   interrupt (what someone else is saying or doing)
     It is not polite to *break in on* what another person is saying.
     He *broke in on* my studying.

break . . . *off* . . .   **broke off**   [**have**] **broken off**   (S)
   end, stop before final decisions are reached, postpone
     The two young men started a conversation, but Dave *broke* it *off* to go to class.

butt *in*   **butted in**   [**have**] **butted in**   (I)
   interrupt, speak before someone else has finished, speak or act in someone else's
   affairs (informal)
     He *butted in* every time she tried to tell a story.
     Don't *butt in* when something does not concern you.

chime *in*   **chimed in**   [**have**] **chimed in**   (I)
   add something (usually in agreeing) to what has just been said
     When Jim started to describe an accident, Jane *chimed in* to give a few other details.

cry *out*   **cried out**   [**have**] **cried out**   (I)
   exclaim, speak or yell in pain or excitement
     George hit his finger with a hammer. "Ouch!" he *cried out.*

go *on* and *on*   **went on and on**   [**have**] **gone on and on**   (I)
   continue (speaking or something else) for a long time
     The speaker tonight *went on and on.*

shout . . . *down* . . .   **shouted down**   [**have**] **shouted down**   (S)
   shout so that someone else cannot be heard
     A crowd should listen to a speaker and should not *shout* him or her *down.*

***speak* about ____**   **spoke about**   [**have**] **spoken about**   (NS)
   talk concerning, mention (=*speak of*)
     Helen and Tom were *speaking about* the football game.

***speak* for ____**   **spoke for**   [**have**] **spoken for**   (NS)
   talk in favor of
     Mrs. Ray *spoke for* lower taxes on food.

***speak* of ____**   **spoke of**   [**have**] **spoken of**   (NS)
   talk concerning, make mention of (=*speak about*)
     Did anyone *speak of* the new history course?

speak *out*   **spoke out**   [have] **spoken out**   (I)
    say publicly (frankly, boldly) what one believes
        Everyone was afraid to *speak out*.

talk *back* to _____   **talked back to**   [have] **talked back to**   (NS)
    answer (especially in a disrespectful or contradictory manner)
        Some children *talk back to* their parents.

talk *down* to _____   **talked down to**   [have] **talked down to**   (NS)
    talk to (another person) as an inferior
        The owner of the store sometimes *talked down to* the clerks.

talk *on* and *on*   **talked on and on**   [have] **talked on and on**   (I)
    talk for a long time
        I don't like people who *talk on and on* about unimportant things.

talk . . . *out* of . . .   **talked out of**   [have] **talked out of**   (S)
    persuade (someone) not to do something (requires two objects)
        Edna *talked* Jane *out of* going to the dance.

talk . . . *up* . . .   **talked up**   [have] **talked up**   (S)
    speak in favor of, praise, urge that (something be done)
        Some students were *talking up* a trip to the game in Florida.

***tell* . . . on . . .**   **told on**   [have] **told on**   (S)
    tell (someone) about a bad action of (someone else) (often takes two objects)
        Sally spilled some milk. Billy *told on* her. (Billy *told* his mother *on* her.)

***think* of _____**   **thought of**   [have] **thought of**   (NS)
    remember, bring to one's mind
        Have you *thought of* that man's name yet?

***touch* on _____**   **touched on**   [have] **touched on**   (NS)
    mention, say a little about, discuss very briefly
        One speaker *touched on* the subject of women's rights.

EXERCISES

1. Reading

Read "Speaking About Speaking" several times. Be ready to read it aloud with a partner, with one person as Helen and the other as Maria.

2. Answering Questions

Answer each question with a complete sentence. Use a correct form of the two- or three-word verb in parentheses. Refer to "Speaking About Speaking" whenever necessary.

> EXAMPLE: What do you do if you say only a few words about something?
> (touch on) *You touch on it.* _____

1. What do you do when you speak of a person? (speak about) _____

2. What verb has the same meaning as *speak about*? (speak of) _____

3. What do you do when you speak in favor of something? (speak for) _____

4. If you answer someone in a not very respectful way, what do you do? (talk back to) _____

5. If you speak to a person as inferior to you, what do you do? (talk down to) _____

6. What is another verb that means "speak in favor of"? (talk up) _____

7. What is another verb that has about the same meaning as *interrupt*? (break in) _____

8. What does a person do who interrupts a conversation? (break in on ___) _____

9. What does a person do who ends a conversation? (break . . . off . . .) _____

10. What may you do if someone hurts or excites you? (cry out) _____

11. What do you do when you say something very suddenly? (blurt . . . out . . .) _____

12. What may an impolite crowd do while you are speaking?   (shout . . . down . . .)   _____

_____

13. What are you doing when you say frankly and publicly what you believe?   (speak out)   _____

_____

14. If you say a little about something, what do you do?   (touch on ___)   _____

_____

15. When you remember or bring something new to your mind, what do you do?   (think of ___)   __

_____

16. If you tell your father that your little sister broke a dish, what do you do?   (tell . . . on . . .)   _____

_____

17. When you and someone else talk for a long time, what do you do?   (talk on and on)   _____

_____

18. If a conversation or something else continues for a long time, what does it do?   (go on and on)   ____

_____

3. Using Verbs in Other Contexts

Choose the verb that better fits the meaning of the sentence.

1. At last night's lecture the speaker _____ solar energy for a long time.   (spoke about, touched on)

2. While he was speaking, I _____ the ways people have wasted other kinds of energy.   (thought of, told on)

3. Some impolite people in the audience did not like what the speaker said. They even tried to _____ him _____ .   (blurt out, shout down)

4. Other people, however, _____ his remarks by clapping.   (broke in on, talked out of)

5. Some people thought that the speaker talked too long. It is true that he _____ .   (chimed in, talked on and on)

6. I admire and respect people who say what they believe. I myself am often afraid to _____ .   (cry out, speak out)

7. Some people, however, speak without thinking. They just _____ whatever occurs to them.   (blurt out, talk out of)

8. Others speak to me as if I were only a child. I don't like people who _____ me like that.   (talk back to, talk down to)

9. Last night's speaker also favored the use of some kinds of weeds to make fuel. In fact, he _____ that _____ very strongly.   (spoke out, talk up)

10. Several of us discussed the speech afterward. We did not _____ until midnight.   (break in, break off)

OTHER MEANINGS OF TWO-WORD VERBS

Many two-word verbs have more than one meaning. Sometimes those meanings are very different.

For example, earlier in this book you have seen *make . . . up . . .* used with different meanings in sentences similar to these:

Tom *made up* an examination. (Chapter 1)
Edna *made up* the beds. (Chapter 3)
Tom *made up* ten meters in his race with Dave. (Chapter 12)
The author *made up* an exciting story. (Chapter 13)

Also, some people *make up* their faces when they put on powder or other cosmetics. After a quarrel, people usually *make up*; that is, they become friendly again.

4. Figuring Out Other Meanings

In the first sentence in each pair below, the italicized verb has a meaning that was given earlier in this book. The second sentence uses the verb in a way that has not been explained. Guess what the verb in the second sentence means and write your answer.

EXAMPLE: A car *backed out* of the garage.
Mr. Jackson and Mr. Clay agreed on a price, but then Mr. Clay *backed out* and would not pay it.

did not keep the agreement, broke his promise

1. Dave's friends told him that they always *backed* him *up* in races.
    Jim *backed* the car *up* to the door.

    _____

2. She asked, "When will—" "I don't know," he *broke in*.
    While the family was away, burglars *broke in* and stole a television set.

    _____

3. The two men talked for a while, but then they *broke off* their discussion.
    Henry *broke off* a small branch from a tree.

    _____

4. Mr. Jackson *called for* the weekly meeting of the family.
    The recipe in that cookbook *called for* two cups of flour for the cake.

    _____

5. The weather *cooled off*. The temperature went down to 50° F.
    The two boys became angry and started to fight, but they soon *cooled off*.

    _____

6. The alarm clock *went off* at six o'clock.
    The gun *went off* accidentally and made a hole in the wall.

    _____

7. Jack is sad because his wife *passed away* last week.
   Remember that if trouble comes, it will finally *pass away*.

   _____

8. Our team *shut out* the other team 8 to 0.
   She closed the door to *shut out* the noises from the street.

   _____

9. We *subscribe to* a magazine called *Newsweek*, which comes each Monday.
   Do you *subscribe to* the belief that the world's population must become smaller?

   _____

10. Jane *washed* her stockings *out* and hung them up to dry.
    The high waters of the flood *washed out* a bridge. Cars could no longer go across.

    _____

11. My brother *worked out* in the gymnasium almost every day.
    Everyone has problems, but usually they *work* them *out* rather well.

    _____

5. Making Up Original Sentences

From this chapter's glossary choose all the verbs that you do not know very well. Make up an original sentence with each.

_____

_____

_____

_____

_____

_____

_____

_____

_____

_____

_____

_____

_____

_____

_____

15. Thinking and Remembering

Looking Back and Looking Forward

It was December 31, New Year's Eve. The five members of the Jackson family were *looking **back** on* the past year and *looking **forward** to* the next year.

"I sometimes *think over* what has been happening to us," George said. "It has *occurred to* me that I would not want to change very much of it."

"I agree," said Edna. "We all *put* our heads *together* and made some important decisions. We have all *attended to* our jobs. I'm glad that Tom did not *pass up* the chance to go to college, and Jane and Jim are *growing up* fast. They have even learned to *put* their clothes *away*!"

"I'm glad that the business is *holding up* well," Tom added. Then he laughed. "I'm also glad that finally I can *tell* the twins *apart* even when they dress alike and cut their hair alike."

Jim said seriously, "It's the rest of the world that scares me. When I *turn over* in my mind all the crime and all the selfishness, and when I hear all the bad news on television, I get worried."

"So do I," said Jane. "We keep ***hearing about*** the possibility of terrible wars. If nations could only *rule out* wars forever, everybody in the world could be happier and better fed."

"You are certainly right," their father said. "But we must *allow for* human weaknesses, which *bring about* most of the world's troubles. Maybe we are moving slowly in the right direction, however. When I *think **back*** to the old times I once studied in history, I remember how cruel many people were then, too."

"I don't know," said Edna. "If we don't *watch out*, somebody will *set off* a war that will *do away with* everything and everybody. But maybe we can *keep on putting off* such an awful event."

"We're all much too serious," George said. "This is New Year's Eve! Let's *cheer up* and help to *ring in* the best new year ever!"

GLOSSARY

INFINITIVE	PAST TENSE	PAST PARTICIPLE	
al*low* for _____	**allowed for**	[**have**] **allowed for**	(NS)

consider, take into consideration, make adjustments because of
    All athletic teams must *allow for* the possibility of injuries.

at*tend* to _____	**attended to**	[**have**] **attended to**	(NS)

take care of, pay attention to
    Attend to your business every day.

bring . . . *about* . . .	**brought about**	[**have**] **brought about**	(S)

cause to happen
    Modern medicine has *brought about* a longer average life span.

cheer *up*   (See Chapter 10)

do a*way* with _____	**did away with**	[**have**] **done away with**	(NS)

destroy, kill, eliminate, get rid of
    Medical research has almost *done away with* smallpox and polio.

grow *up*	**grew up**	[**have**] **grown up**	(I)

become mature, become an adult
    I wish those children would *grow up*.

hear about _____	**heard about**	[**have**] **heard about**	(NS)

learn of, get news or information about
    How did you *hear about* the new medicine?

hold *up*	**held up**	[**have**] **held up**	(I)

continue in a satisfactory way (a business, some other endeavor, or a machine, etc.)
    The profits of the company are *holding up* well.

keep on _____   (See Chapter 2)

look *back* on _____   (See Chapter 6)

look *forward* to _____	**looked forward to**	[**have**] **looked forward to**	(NS)

expect with pleasure, think about (future events)
    The Jacksons *look forward* hopefully *to* a time of world peace.

oc*cur* to _____	**occurred to**	[**have**] **occurred to**	(NS)

come to the mind of, suggest itself to (usually in the phrase *occurred* [or *occurs*]
to, followed by a clause starting with *that*)
    It *occurred to* Tom that the twins' birthday was the next day.

pass . . . *up* . . .	**passed up**	[**have**] **passed up**	(S)

fail to do or take advantage of (something that seems good)
    "Don't *pass up* your chance to save a lot of money," the salesman urged.

put . . . *away* . . .   (See Chapter 2)

put . . . *off* . . .   (See Chapter 1)

put [heads] *together*	**put** [heads] *together*	[**have**] **put** [heads] *together*	(S)

think about together, confer
    Let's *put* our heads *together* and decide what we should do next.

ring . . . *in* . . .   **rang in**   **[have] rung in**   (S)

    ring bells to celebrate the coming of (In many places, bells are rung on New Year's Eve.)

        A group of students *rang in* the New Year at the church.

rule . . . *out* . . .   **ruled out**   **[have] ruled out**   (S)

    exclude, not permit

        Almost everyone hopes that wars can be *ruled out* forever.

set . . . *off* . . .   **set off**   **[have] set off**   (S)

    cause to start, explode (something)

        Only trained workers should *set off* dynamite or other explosives.

tell . . . *apart* . . .   **told apart**   **[have] told apart**   (S)

    identify either when both are present, distinguish one from another

        George cannot *tell* the two kittens *apart*.

think *back*   **thought back**   **[have] thought back**   (I)

    remember, think of past events

        George and Edna *thought back* to the early days of their business.

think . . . *over* . . .   **thought over**   **[have] thought over**   (S)

    think seriously about, think about again

        They *thought over* what they might have done differently.

turn . . . *over* . . .   **turned over**   **[have] turned over**   (S)

    look at from various angles (in one's mind), think about in various ways

        They *turned over* the possibilities for the future.

watch *out*   **watched out**   **[have] watched out**   (I)

    be careful (often as a warning in the form *Watch out*. *Look out* has the same meaning.

    Look out [*for*] has a similar meaning. It is used if the danger is very near:

    Look out for that truck!)

        If you drive today, *watch out*. The streets are wet and slippery.

EXERCISES

1. Reading

Read "Looking Back and Looking Forward" several times. If possible, read the conversation aloud with four other persons. Each may read what is said by George, Edna, Tom, Jim, or Jane.

2. Choosing the Right Verb

From each group of verbs choose the one that fits best in each sentence. Write the form that should be used.

allow for   attend to   cheer up   grow up   hear about

1. In school a good student _____ every assignment.

2. Edna was sad, but George asked her to _____ .

3. Have you _____ the newest cars?

4. My little sister _____ during the five years I was away.

5. When you buy cloth to make a skirt, you must _____ the cloth that will be wasted.

pass up   hold up   look back on   look forward to   occur to

6. It _____ me last night that Roy might be in danger.

7. She is _____ spending the holiday with her family next month.

8. This engine has _____ very well.

9. Sometime in the future you may _____ this year as a very happy one.

10. Yesterday Edna _____ a chance to work in a bakery.

put away   put . . . together   put off   ring in   look out

11. Let's _____ our heads _____ and solve the problem.

12. Children often do not _____ their toys _____ .

13. Some people _____ washing dishes until all of them are dirty.

14. As usual, the members of the church _____ the New Year at midnight on December 31.

15. _____ ! A car is coming!

rule out   tell apart   think back   think over   turn over   watch out

16. Fred sat there and _____ several possibilities _____ in his mind.

17. If you look very carefully at two peas, you can _____ them _____ .

18. _____ ! That gun is loaded!

19. Maybe you should go to school for one more year. Do not _____ that possibility.

20. Rachel drank her coffee and _____ on the events of the past month.

21. _____ it _____ carefully before you decide.

3. Answering Questions

Write a complete sentence to answer each of these questions. Use the correct form of the italicized verb. Your answers should tell what you believe. Other people may write different answers to some of the questions.

EXAMPLES: Do you sometimes *think back* to the earlier years of your life? *Yes, I sometimes think back to the past.*

Has it ever *occurred to* you that today is the tomorrow which you were afraid of? *No, that has never occurred to me.*

1. Are you usually sad when you *look back on* the past year? _____

2. Do you like to *look forward to* next year? _____

3. If you and someone else *put* your heads *together*, would you bump your heads? _____

4. Do you *attend to* your work carefully? _____

5. Firecrackers explode with a loud noise. Have you ever *set off* firecrackers? _____

6. When you see twins, can you usually *tell* them *apart*? _____

7. Do you believe that you have *grown up* yet? _____

8. When did you first *hear about* this English class? _____

9. Why are you studying English? What *brought about* your decision? _____

10. Did you *think* it *over* before you began taking English? _____

11. Have you ever *rung in* a new year? _____

12. Have you ever *passed up* a chance to make a great deal of money? _____

_____

13. Do you often *put off* your work? _____

_____

14. Do *Look out*! and *Watch out*! have similar meanings? _____

_____

15. Jane said that wars should be *ruled out* forever. Do you agree with her? _____

_____

REVERSED PAIRS

Sometimes the two parts of two-word verbs appear in reverse order as one-word verbs. These usually have very different meanings.

For example, *hold . . . up . . .* (Chapter 6) means "to rob" and *hold up* (Chapter 15) may mean "continue in a satisfactory way." But *uphold* often means "confirm" or "give moral or legal support to": The Supreme Court *upheld* what the lower courts had decided.

Here are some of the other common verbs of this kind.

TWO-WORD VERB	COMMON MEANING AND EXAMPLE	ONE-WORD VERB	COMMON MEANING AND EXAMPLE
come over	come to one's home	**overcome**	conquer, win against (someone or something)
"My friend is *coming over* soon," she said.		George *overcame* a childhood disease.	
do over	do again, repeat	**overdo**	do too much (of)
Tom made a mistake and had to *do* the problem *over*		Dave *overdid* his exercise and hurt some muscles.	
look over	inspect, examine	**overlook**	fail to see, fail to pay attention to
George was *looking over* a damaged mower.		Don't *overlook* the figures on page 26.	
run over	drive across the top of	**overrun**	spread over (usually harmfully)
The speeding driver *ran over* a dog.		The army *overran* most of the countryside.	
sell out	sell all of	**outsell**	sell more than (someone), have more sold than (something)
The store *sold out* its Christmas candy.		Each salesman likes to *outsell* the others. Potatoes *outsell* turnips.	
set in	begin	**inset**	put in, fasten in
Cold weather was *setting in*.		He *inset* small pieces of metal to make a pretty design.	
set up	start, establish	**upset**	tip over, turn on the side or upside down
They *set up* their shop on Vincent Street.		The wagon *upset* in the road.	

TWO-WORD VERB	COMMON MEANING AND EXAMPLE	ONE-WORD VERB	COMMON MEANING AND EXAMPLE
take over	take charge of	**overtake**	catch up with

When George was away, Edna *took over* management of the business.

Tom *overtook* Helen on the way to class.

Turn over and *overturn*, however, mean the same thing, "to upset."

4. Choosing the Right Verb

Which verb from each group fits best in each sentence? Use the correct form.

overdo   overlook   overrun   overtake   outsell

1. Don't _____ the possibility that you have made a mistake.

2. Thousands of hungry insects _____ my garden last summer, eating most of my vegetables.

3. Dave started out ahead in the race, but Tom _____ him.

4. Sugar _____ salt in today's food stores.

5. Exercise is good, but don't _____ it.

overcome   overturn   upset   inset   uphold

6. Be careful not to _____ my flower pot.

7. You can make an attractive pattern if you _____ pieces of wood just below the surface.

8. Ray had only one hand, but he _____ this problem by using a metal hook skillfully.

9. Because the road was covered with ice, the car slid off and _____ .

10. When children argue, a parent must sometimes _____ the opinion of one of them.

5. Making Up Original Sentences

Make up an original sentence with each of the ten verbs listed in Exercise 4.

_____

_____

_____

_____

_____

_____

_____

_____

_____

_____

6. Making Up an Original Conversation

Read once more "Looking Back and Looking Forward." Think about a conversation that you and some of your friends might have on the last day of the year. Use at least eight of the two-word and three-word verbs in this chapter's glossary.

_____

_____

_____

_____

_____

_____

_____

_____

_____

_____

_____

_____

_____

_____

_____

_____

_____

Cumulative Review

REVIEW EXERCISES I

This is a review of some of the verbs in Chapters 1—5.

1. Using Objects of Separable Verbs

Here are some parts of sentences with S verbs. Where may each object shown in parentheses be placed? Remember that a pronoun such as *it* or *them* may only separate the two-word verb.

You may write the three possible answers or give them orally, as your teacher prefers.

EXAMPLE: Jim *checked over*. (his paper, it)

Jim checked over his paper.
Jim checked his paper over.
Jim checked it over.

1. Let's *check over*. (our papers, them)

_____

_____

_____

2. He *crossed out*. (it, a wrong answer)

_____

_____

_____

3. We *found out*. (it, the truth)

_____

_____

_____

4. We should *look up*. (those articles, them)

_____

_____

_____

5. I like to *put together*. (these, puzzles like this)

_____

_____

_____

6. We *gave away*. (them, some food)

_____

_____

_____

7. She *had on*. (some old shoes, them)

_____

_____

_____

8. Jim didn't *hang up*. (his sweater, it)

_____

_____

_____

9. I tried to *pick up*. (them, the dishes)

_____

_____

_____

10. Have they *used up*? (all the soap, it)

_____

_____

_____

11. She *left on*. (her gloves, them)

_____

_____

_____

12. Please *try on*. (these shoes, them)

_____

_____

_____

13. Dave *left out*. (one problem, it)

_____

_____

_____

14. Please *shut off*. (the water, it)

_____

_____

_____

15. Children quickly *wear out*. (their clothes, them)

_____

_____

_____

16. Tom *asked out*. (her, Helen)

_____

_____

_____

17. The committee *put off*. (it, the celebration)

_____

_____

_____

18. Jane *washed out*. (some clothing, it)

_____

_____

_____

19. Edna *wiped off*. (it, the counter)

_____

_____

_____

20. She *left on*. (the radio, it)

_____

_____

_____

2. Using "-ing" Forms

Write an original sentence using the *-ing* form of each verb. Include the words in parentheses also.

EXAMPLE: *go after* (some sandwiches)

I am going after some sandwiches.

1. look for _____ (the cat)

_____

2. get up (I don't like)

_____

3. put . . . away . . . (my books)

_____

4. burn up (That building is)

_____

5. boil over (The milk)

_____

6. sew . . . up . . . (a hole in his pocket)

_____

7. show off (enjoy)

_____

8. hand . . . in . . . (her examination paper)

_____

9. look at _____ (some paintings)

_____

10. turn . . . on . . . (all the lights)

_____

11. dust . . . off . . . (the furniture)

_____

12. cloud up (The sky)

_____

13. come over (soon)

_____

14. wait for _____ (a bus)

_____

15. read through _____ (several newspapers)

_____

160

16. run out of ____ (time)

_____

17. break . . . up . . . (The baby was)

_____

18. sweep . . . out . . . (the shop)

_____

19. live on ____ (bread and water)

_____

20. get together (to discuss their problems)

_____

3. Using Past Participles

Here are sentences with missing verbs. What is the past participle that should be used in each?

EXAMPLE: (find out) I have ____*found out*____ what was wrong.

1. (catch up with) They have _____ us.
2. (give up) She has _____ .
3. (go after) We had recently _____ some stamps.
4. (keep up with) Dave has _____ Pedro.
5. (make up) Helen has _____ the examination _____ .
6. (put in) Edna has _____ several potatoes _____ .
7. (read through) I have _____ the article.
8. (stand for) It must have _____ something else.
9. (tear up) A dog has _____ it _____ .
10. (come across) They have _____ some unusual families.
11. (get up) She has _____ early.
12. (hang up) They have _____ their clothing.
13. (let in) Edna had _____ the cat _____ a few minutes earlier.
14. (run down) The clock has _____ .
15. (see about) Edna had _____ the cat again.
16. (cut up) I have _____ it _____ .
17. (do without) They have _____ any food.
18. (eat up) The children have _____ all the ice cream.
19. (put off) The farmers have _____ buying their seed.

20. (leave on)   They have _____ the lights _____ .

21. (lie down)   She has _____ on the floor.

22. (sit down)   He has _____ on the floor.

23. (blow up)   The tank had _____ a few days before.

24. (grow out of)   Jim has _____ his shirts.

25. (set in)   Winter had _____ early that year.

26. (take up)   The work had _____ two hours of her time.

27. (shut off)   George has _____ the water.

28. (wear out)   Jim has already _____ his coat.

29. (bring about)   High prices have _____ some changes.

30. (show off)   Dave has often _____ .

4. Using Past Tenses

What is the past tense of each verb in Exercise 3? Leave out *have, has, or had* in each sentence. Make other changes if necessary. Write out the new sentence.

EXAMPLE: (find out)   *I found out what was wrong.* _____

1. (catch up with) _____

2. (give up) _____

3. (go after) _____

4. (keep up with) _____

5. (make up) _____

6. (put in) _____

7. (read through) _____

8. (stand for) _____

9. (tear up) _____

10. (come across) _____

11. (get up) _____

12. (hang up) _____

13. (let in) _____

14. (run down) _____

15. (see about) _____

16. (cut up) _____

17. (do without) _____

18. (eat up) _____

19. (put off) _____

20. (leave on) _____

21. (lie down) _____

22. (sit down) _____

23. (blow up) _____

24. (grow out of) _____

25. (set in) _____

26. (take up) _____

27. (shut off) _____

28. (wear out) _____

29. (bring about) _____

30. (show off) _____

REVIEW EXERCISES II

This is a review of some of the verbs in Chapters 6−10.

1. Making Up "Yes-No" Questions

Change each of these sentences into a question that can be answered *yes* or *no*. Use the correct form of the italicized verb. The first word of the question is given.

EXAMPLE: Everyone *filled in* the blanks.

Did *everyone fill in the blanks?*

1. George's father *dropped out* of school. Did _____

_____

2. George's father was sorry that he once *held up* people. Was _____

_____

3. He *settled down* later. Did _____

_____

4. He and his wife usually *pulled together*. Did _____

_____

5. A person should not *go back on* a promise. Should _____

_____

6. Police sometimes *line up* suspected criminals. Do _____

_____

7. A young person must sometimes *look for* a job. Must _____

_____

8. Criminals sometimes *get away*. Do _____

_____

9. The old man's death was *drawing near*. Was _____

_____

10. His wife has always *stood by* him. Has _____

_____

2. Making Up "Wh-" Questions

Change each of these sentences to a *wh-* question. Use the correct form of the italicized verb. The first word of the question is given.

EXAMPLE: The day before Christmas the Jacksons *set out* for Hillsdale.

When *did the Jacksons set out for Hillsdale?*

1. Every Christmas they *headed out* toward Hillsdale. When _____

_____

2. They *turned around* because they had forgotten a present. Why _____

_____

3. Mrs. Jackson had *checked in* at the airport. Where _____

_____

4. The plane had *taken off* an hour late. When _____

_____

5. Edna *dined out* with her parents. Who _____

_____

6. Edna *dined out* with her parents after she arrived. When _____

_____

7. Edna *dined out* with her parents. With whom _____

_____

8. A driver *ran off* the road because he was drunk. Why _____

_____

9. He *ran over* a pile of sand. What _____

_____

10. The Jacksons' right front tire *blew out*. Which _____

_____

3. Using Intransitive Verbs

Make up an original sentence using the *-ing* form of each of these intransitive verbs.

EXAMPLE: (curl up) *The kitten is curling up on the bed.* _____

1. (sign up) _____

2. (work out) _____

3. (pair off) _____

4. (help out) _____

5. (warm up) _____

6. (slip away) _____

Make up an original sentence using the past tense of each of these intransitive verbs.

7. (hang back) _____

8. (take off) _____

9. (break down) _____

10. (cut across) _____

11. (bear down) _____

12. (sit down) _____

13. (go on) _____

14. (get back) _____

15. (go back) _____

16. (follow through) _____

Make up an original sentence using the past participle of each of the verbs listed in 7−16. Use topics that are different from those you wrote about above.

17. (hang back) _____

18. (take off) _____

19. (break down) _____

20. (cut across) _____

21. (bear down) _____

22. (sit down) _____

23. (go on) _____

24. (get back) _____

25. (go back) _____

26. (follow through) _____

4. Varying Placement of Adverbs

Say or write each of the following sentences two times. Put the adverb in a different correct place each time.

1. (carefully)   Helen looked for the mistake.

_____

_____

2. (happily)   The old man looked back on his marriage.

_____

_____

3. (quickly)   Jim jacked up the car.

_____

_____

4. (immediately)   Edna put her coat on.

_____

_____

5. (carelessly)   The driver plowed into a truck.

_____

_____

6. (slowly)   Tom backed out.

_____

_____

7. (steadily)   The noise went on.

_____

_____

8. (skillfully)   George fixed the engine up.

_____

_____

9. (regularly)   The Jacksons had saved up money.

_____

_____

10. (constantly)   Prices were going up.

_____

_____

5.   Using Negatives

Make each of the following sentences negative four times. Use each verb in parentheses with *not* or *n't*. Sometimes you will need to change the form of the two-word verb.

EXAMPLE: (did, may, have, are)   They called off the game.

They did not call off the game.
They may not call off the game.
They have not called off the game.
They are not calling off the game.

1. (could, may, have, are)   We agreed on the terms.

_____

_____

_____

_____

2. (does, did, may, must)   The business pays off.

_____

_____

_____

_____

3. (should, may, is, did)   Mr. Jackson cheered up.

_____

_____

_____

_____

4. (could, would, may, has)   Edna parted with her old dishes.

_____

_____

_____

_____

5. (do, did, may, are)   Some people stick to their work.

_____

_____

_____

_____

6. (does, should, could, did)   Mr. Jackson counted on help from his family.

_____

_____

_____

_____

7. (did, may, could, are)   The Jacksons dined out often.

_____

_____

_____

_____

8. (would, could, must, have)   The Jacksons signed up with a dishonest dealer.

_____

_____

_____

_____

9. (does, will, has, is)   Helen passes out.

_____

_____

_____

_____

10. (did, does, is, has)   She felt up to walking faster.

_____

_____

_____

_____

6. Using Imperatives

Here are some examples of imperative sentences, including some with *please* or negative words, and some in the form of questions.

Sit down. Please sit down. Do sit down. Sit down, please. Will you sit down. Don't sit down. Put your hat on. Put on your hat. Please put your hat on. Please put on your hat. Will you put on your hat. Will you please put on your hat. Please don't put on your hat.

What are three (or more) other ways in which each of these commands or requests may be said?

1. Cheer up. _____

_____

Name _____ Section _____ Date _____

2. Pay off your debts. _____
    _____

3. Do the problem over. _____
    _____

4. Don't back out of the agreement. _____
    _____

5. Do not turn down my offer. _____
    _____

6. Turn around. _____
    _____

7. Get into the car. _____
    _____

8. Ring for the nurse. _____
    _____

9. Try out for the band, Joe. _____
    _____

10. Take your shoes off. _____
    _____

REVIEW EXERCISES III

This is a review of some of the verbs in Chapters 11−15.

1. Placing Objects

Where should each object be placed?

EXAMPLE:

Susan made up { several very exciting stories / them / some stories.

Susan made up several very interesting stories.
Susan made them up.
Susan made some stories up.
Susan made up some stories

1.

Tom nosed out
$\begin{cases} \text{all the other runners in the race} \\ \text{them} \\ \text{the other runners} \end{cases}$

_____

_____

_____

_____

2.

George thought over
$\begin{cases} \text{it} \\ \text{his problem} \\ \text{what he could do to make the shop larger} \end{cases}$

_____

_____

_____

_____

3.

Edna handed out
$\begin{cases} \text{them} \\ \text{some gifts for the small children} \\ \text{several gifts} \end{cases}$

_____

_____

_____

_____

4.

Edna summed up
$\begin{cases} \text{everybody's opinion} \\ \text{what everyone in the room was thinking} \\ \text{it} \end{cases}$

_____

_____

_____

_____

5.
    The Jacksons may put up   { a larger building than they now have
                                                 a larger building
                                                 it

_____

_____

_____

_____

2. Using the Passive Voice

Change each of these sentences to make the verb and the sentence form passive.

EXAMPLE: The Jacksons kept their expenses down as much as possible.
Their expenses were kept down as much as possible.

1. They marked their prices down. _____

_____

2. They handed out free pencils. _____

_____

3. We must count up all the pencils. _____

_____

4. A team from Pennsylvania carried off the first prize. _____

_____

5. The Pennsylvanians shut out our team for ten minutes. _____

_____

6. Soldiers successfully fought off a few rebels. _____

_____

7. Students using this book make up many original sentences. _____

_____

8. Jim and Jane have written up a summary of the class discussion. _____

_____

9. People in the audience blurted out some unpleasant remarks. _____

_____

10. We must rule out the use of guns. _____

_____

3. Using "-ing" Forms As Objects

Finish each of these sentences by adding any *-ing* word that makes sense. Add any other necessary words.

EXAMPLE: Edna planned on *working late.* _____

1.   After graduating, I hope to engage in   _____

2.   We kept on   _____

3.   Did they feel like   _____

4.   They had planned on   _____

5.   The people in the audience went on   _____

6.   I have never succeeded in   _____

7.   Most people do not figure on   _____

8.   Please try to put up with my   _____

9.   Since no water was left, we had to do without   _____ for almost a day.

10.   It is not easy to face up to   _____

4. Using Nouns Made from Two-Word Verbs

Review the nouns that have been made from two-word verbs (Chapter 12, page 127). Choose ten of them, and make up an original sentence with each.

_____

_____

_____

_____

_____

_____

_____

_____

_____

_____

Answer Key

CHAPTER 1

1. Reading

Oral work

2. Using Past Tenses and Past Participles

1. caught up with
   have caught up with
2. checked over
   has checked over
3. fell behind
   has fallen behind
4. found out
   has found out
5. got away from
   has got (*or* gotten) away from
6. gave up
   has given up
7. went after
   have gone after
8. handed their papers in
   have handed their papers in
9. kept at
   has kept at
10. made up
    has made up
11. put off
    have put off
12. stood for
    have stood for
13. tore the cloth up
    has torn the cloth up
14. tried out their plan on
    have tried out their plan on
15. turned his assignment in
    has turned his assignment in

3. Substituting

1. heading for
2. caught up with
3. going after
4. look for
5. checking over
6. found out
7. put in
8. look up
9. read through
10. keeping up with
11. falling behind
12. put off
13. tore up
14. trying out (I've been *trying out* some new ideas on Maria.)

4. Substituting

1. hand the paper in
2. brush up on
3. figure out
4. stand for
5. make up
6. turned in
7. cross them off
8. put together
9. give up
10. pull through
11. get along
12. keep at
13. get away

5. Practicing Pronunciation

Oral work

6. Using Separable Verbs

1. Nina checks over each paper.
   Nina checks each paper over.
   Nina checks it over.
2. Hedda tore up several pages.
   Hedda tore several pages up.
   Hedda tore them up.
3. She figured them out.
   She figured the answers out.
   She figured out the answers.

4. Dave looked up an old magazine.
   Dave looked an old magazine up.
   Dave looked it up.
5. Tom made up a test on Tuesday.
   Tom made a test up on Tuesday.
   Tom made it up on Tuesday.
6. He had turned it in on Monday.
   He had turned his paper in on Monday.
   He had turned in his paper on Monday.

7. He made a list of assignments and crossed off the items one by one.
   He made a list of assignments and crossed the items off one by one.
   He made a list of assignments and crossed them off one by one.
8. Lee disliked studying, and he kept putting it off.
   Lee disliked studying, and he kept putting his history lesson off.
   Lee disliked studying, and he kept putting off his history lesson.
9. He handed in his paper late.
   He handed his paper in late.
   He handed it in late.
10. Tom put it together.
    Tom put a list together.
    Tom put together a list.

7. Making Up Original Sentences

Answers will vary.

CHAPTER 2

1. Reading

Oral work

2. Substituting

1. goes off
2. turn it off
3. gives up
4. run down
5. turns on

6. get up
7. keeps on
8. sits up
9. stands up
10. puts a bathrobe on

11. goes in
12. plugs in
13. used up
14. pop up
15. lets the cat out

3. Substituting

1. have on (Jim asks Jane, "What in the world do you *have on*?")
2. wash out
3. hunt up
4. given away

5. get into
6. running out of
7. feel like (I don't *feel like* listening to another argument.)
8. put away
9. hang your clothes up
10. come across
11. let us in (You should *let* us *in* on whatever is funny.)
12. looking at
13. care for
14. sees about, lets it in
15. pick up
16. sets out

4. Using Past Tense Forms

3. gave up
5. turned on
7. kept on
8. sat up
9. stood up
10. put a bathrobe on

11. went in
12. plugged in
15. let the cat out

. . .

14. saw about, let it in
15. picked up
16. set out

5. Using Past Participles

3. has given up
5. has turned on
7. has kept on
8. has sat up
9. has stood up
10. has put a bathrobe on

11. has gone in
12. has plugged in
15. has let the cat out

. . .

14. has seen about, has let it in
15. have picked up
16. has set out

6. Making Up Pantomimes

Pantomime

7. Answering Questions

1. went off
2. put on
3. sat up
4. plugged in, plugged it in
5. used up, used them up
6. pops up
7. let the cat out, let it out
8. wash her clothes out, wash them out

9. had on
10. running out of
11. put away, put them away
12. hang her clothes up, hang them up
13. care for, care for
14. let the cat in, let it in
15. picked up, picked them up

8. Making Up Original Sentences

Answers will vary.

CHAPTER 3

1. Reading

Oral work

2. Answering Questions

1. turns on, turns it on
2. going on
3. cleans up, cleans it up
4. clears the table off, washes up, wipes off, rubs off, mops up
5. leaves the radio on, leaves it on
6. boiled over
7. air out
8. made them up, made up
9. hung up
10. plugged it up
11. opens the drain up, opens it up
12. straightens up
13. calls up
14. calls back
15. cut them off
16. sits down
17. makes out
18. eat everything up
19. stock up on
20. do without
21. dress up
22. tries them on
23. picks out, looks over
24. lie down, doze off
25. cuts up

3. Using Verbs with "Up"

Oral work

4. Using Verbs with "Off" and "Out"

Oral work

5. Making Up Pantomimes

Pantomime

6. Making Up Original Sentences

Answers will vary.

CHAPTER 4

1. Reading

Oral work

2. Substituting

1. came back
2. clouding up, cooling off
3. coming up
4. warm up
5. set in
6. snow us in
7. clear off
8. put in
9. lived on
10. blew up
11. left out
12. kept up
13. talked about

3. Substituting

1. shut off
2. dry off
3. called for
4. talked about
5. worn out
6. grown out of
7. let down (Edna said, "Maybe I can *let down* the hem in my blue dress.")
8. part with
9. talking over
10. sewed up
11. took up
12. turn in

4. Using the "-ing" Form

1. coming back
2. warming up
3. setting in
4. living on
5. keeping the conversation up
6. talking about
7. sewing up
8. looking at
9. turning off
10. turning in

5. Using Past Participles

1. blown up
2. come back
3. come up
4. dried off
5. grown out of
6. left out
7. let down

6. Trying Variations

Answers will vary.

7. Making Up Original Sentences

Answers will vary.

CHAPTER 5

1. Reading

Oral work

2. Answering Questions

1. showed up
2. get along
3. came over
4. drop in
5. bumped into
6. made up
7. walked out on
8. put up with
9. teamed up
10. ran across
11. look in on
12. run into

3. Answering Questions

1. waiting on
2. ask her out
3. take her out
4. warm up to
5. stop by
6. get together
7. wait for
8. brought them up
9. called her up
10. turned it down
11. put it off

4. Asking "Yes-No" Questions

1. Are Tom and Pedro coming over?
2. Did Susan and Don make up?
3. Have Susan and Don made up?
4. Did Tom run into Susan?
5. Is Susan trying to show off?
6. Should we wait for our friends to come?
7. Can we get together for a picnic?
8. Does Maria call Susan up?
9. Have the friends put off the party?
10. Did Susan and Don turn us down?
11. Can nations, like people, make up when they disagree?
12. Should national leaders bring up new ideas for a peaceful world?
13. Can nations get along together?
14. Should nations team up to fight hunger and disease?
15. Must all of us put up with the "strange" customs and beliefs of other countries?

5. Asking "Wh-" Questions

1. When did Tom and Pedro show up at Helen and Maria's apartment?
2. How often do they show up there?
3. Where did Tom run into Susan?
4. Who ran into Susan?
5. Whom did Tom run into?
6. Whom was Susan waiting on?
7. When did the eight students get together for a picnic?
8. When are Susan and Don coming over?
9. Who may put off the party?
10. What may Don put off?
11. When did Susan and Don stop by?
12. Who else dropped in?
13. Why did they stop by?
14. How do Helen and Tom get along?
15. Why do Helen and Tom get along well?

6. Making Up Original Sentences

Answers will vary.

CHAPTER 6

1. Reading

Oral work

2. Substituting

1. passed away
2. drifted off
3. sat up with
4. drawing near
5. faced up to
6. tried out for
7. dropped out of
8. fell in with
9. held up (We *held up* people.)
10. line up
11. called in
12. pick out
13. got away
14. let on
15. got out of

3. Substituting

1. go back
2. go back on
3. met with
4. let me off
5. looked for
6. fell for
7. settle down
8. stood by
9. hung back
10. look back on
11. pulled together
12. hold back
13. rang for

4. Pronouncing Three-Word Verbs

Answers will vary.

5. Using Three-Word Verbs

1. run out of
2. stock up on
3. gets out of
4. falls in with
5. dropped out of
6. tried out for
7. put up with
8. face up to
9. goes back on
10. look back on
11. catch up with
12. sitting up with

6. Completing Sentences

1. away
2. away
3. back
4. up
5. for
6. for
7. for
8. by
9. together
10. down
11. in
12. up
13. off
14. near
15. back
16. on
17. with
18. back
19. off
20. out

7. Making Up Original Sentences

Answers will vary.

CHAPTER 7

1. Reading

Oral work

2. Answering Questions

1. The Jackson family got into their car and set out.
2. Tom headed out toward the highway.
3. The neighbors' dog saw them off.
4. He turned around because the twins had forgotten their present.
5. Jane got out after they got back to the house.
6. Yes, she got in again.
7. Tom backed out of the driveway.
8. No, she checked in early.
9. Yes, she got on without waiting long.
10. She got on the plane without waiting.
11. He husband sent her off with flowers.
12. He let down the wheels.
13. No, there wasn't any trouble when the plane headed into the unloading area.
14. She saw her father and mother when she got off the plane.
15. They dined out at a lovely restaurant.
16. A drunken driver cut in ahead of them.
17. Yes, he was weaving in and out.
18. Yes, he ran off the road.
19. No, he ran over a pile of sand and plowed into a parked truck.
20. Tom pulled over to see whether the driver was hurt.
21. A policeman came up after a few minutes.
22. Yes, he was afraid that it might break down.
23. No, the right front tire blew out.
24. Everybody piled out.
25. He jacked up the front end.
26. Tom took off the tire, and Jim put the spare tire on.
27. No, he had not figured on a blowout.
28. They pulled in an hour late.

3. Pronouncing Intransitive Verbs

Oral work

4. Using Intransitive Verbs

1. coming up, came up, come up, come up
2. get back, got back, got (or gotten) back
3. blew out, blow out, blown out
4. taking off, take off, took off, taken off
5. set out, setting out, set out, set out

5. Using Adverbs with Two-Word Verbs

(The adverb may be moved to any place marked by a caret ˄ .)

1. ˄ The family ˄ got in .
2. ˄ A policeman ˄ came up .
3. ˄ We checked in at the hotel ˄ .
4. ˄ The drunken driver cut in ˄ .
5. ˄ Tom turned around ˄ .
6. ˄ The pilot let the wheels down ˄ .
   ˄ The pilot ˄ let down the wheels ˄ .
7. ˄ Tom took off his coat ˄ .
   ˄ Tom ˄ took his coat off ˄ .

8. ˄ Jim put the spare wheel on ˄ .
   ˄ Jim ˄ put on the spare wheel ˄ .
9. ˄ Jane turned down the invitation ˄ .
   ˄ Jane ˄ turned the invitation down ˄ .
10. ˄ Edna cleared the table off ˄ .
    ˄ Edna ˄ cleared off the table ˄ .
11. ˄ The driver ran over a pile of sand ˄ .
12. ˄ One woman ˄ got ˄ off the bus .
13. ˄ The rider headed ˄ into the water ˄ .

14. ˄ George ˄ rang for the nurse ˄ .
15. ˄ Many people meet ˄ with their lawyers ˄ .
16. ˄ George ˄ sat up with his father .
17. ˄ The old man looked ˄ back on his married life ˄ .
18. ˄ Roy goes back ˄ on his promise .
19. ˄ Jack got ˄ out of jail ˄ .
20. ˄ Susan faced up ˄ to the new problems ˄ .

6. Using Verbs with "Get"

1. got in
2. got out
3. got on
4. got back
5. got off
6. get together (*or* got together)
7. get away from
8. get along
9. get into
10. get up
11. got out of
12. got away
13. gets ahead
14. get ahead of
15. gets behind
16. get through
17. get down
18. got over

7. Making Up an Original Composition

Answers will vary.

CHAPTER 8

1. Reading

Oral work

2. Substituting

1. work out
2. slipping away
3. feel up to (Helen said, "I wouldn't *feel up to* doing this every day.")
4. worn myself out

5.	keep up	13.	hold on
6.	pass out	14.	warming up
7.	black out	15.	go on
8.	curl up	16.	move on
9.	sit down	17.	cut out for
10.	catch up with	18.	asks for
11.	pointed out	19.	follow up
12.	cut across	20.	follow through

3. Using Negatives

1. Helen does not slip away from the others.
   Helen will not slip away from the others.
   Helen may not slip away from the others.
   Helen must not slip away from the others.
2. Helen and Maria cannot catch up with their friends.
   Helen and Maria should not catch up with their friends.
   Helen and Maria did not catch up with their friends.
   Helen and Maria ought not to catch up with their friends.
3. Helen did not curl up in the leaves.
   Helen has not curled up in the leaves.
   Helen should not curl up in the leaves.
   Helen might not curl up in the leaves.
4. Tom is not following through when he swings his tennis racket.
   Tom does not follow through when he swings his tennis racket.
   Tom must not follow through when he swings his tennis racket.
   Tom may not follow through when he swings his tennis racket.
5. Dave did not point out Tom's mistake.
   Dave will not point out Tom's mistake.
   Dave has not pointed out Tom's mistake.
   Dave ought not to point out Tom's mistake.
6. Maria does not sit down.
   Maria had not sat down.
   Maria is not sitting down.
   Maria must not sit down.
7. They do not go on.
   They have not gone on.
   They are not going on.
   They may not go on.
8. They did not cut across a farmer's pasture.
   They must not cut across a farmer's pasture.
   They should not cut across the farmer's pasture.
   They would not cut across a farmer's pasture.
9. Sigrid does not work out daily.
   Sigrid was not working out daily.
   Sigrid has not worked out daily.
   Sigrid should not work out daily.
10. Helen did not feel up to walking a long distance.
    Helen has not felt up to walking a long distance.
    Helen may not feel up to walking a long distance.
    Helen will not feel up to walking a long distance.

4. Using Imperatives

1. Sit down.
2. Please sit down.
3. Sit down, please.
4. Get into the car.
5. Please get into the car.
6. Get into the car, please.
7. Will you stand up, please.
8. Will you please stand up.
9. Don't cut across the grass.
10. Please don't cut across the grass.
11. Slip away early, please.
12. Take off your hat.
13. Please take it off.
14. Take it off, please.
15. Will you please take your hat off.
    (*or* Will you please take off your hat.)

5. Making Up Original Sentences

Answers will vary.

CHAPTER 9

1. Reading

Oral work

2. Answering Questions

(Slight differences in answers are possible.)

1. He could fix it up.
2. They talked over the possibility of setting up their own business.
3. He planned on having his own business.
4. He would go into business much earlier.
5. They have paid them off.
6. They have saved up a little money.
7. It laid them off.
8. Sales slackened off.
9. He sent for George Jackson.
10. They had dropped off.
11. She promised to help out with the selling and the accounts.
12. No, building up a business is not often easy.
13. They inch along.
14. Yes, he believes that they can live on it.
15. He will tune them up.
16. They could take it over.
17. He wanted George to sign up at once.
18. He wanted to talk it over with his wife.
19. He might hold out for more rent.
20. He thought an agreement might be worked out.
21. She thought that they should sleep on it.

3. Using Verbs in Other Contexts

1. drop off
2. lays off
3. live on
4. save up
5. Setting up
6. sleep on
7. build up
8. work out
9. help out
10. do the work over
11. send for
12. pay off
13. slacken off
14. take over
15. plan on

4. Using Long Objects with Separable Verbs

1. George could fix up old engines. (*or* . . . fix old engines up)
   George could fix them up.
   George could fix up an old engine that no one else could repair.
2. George and Edna talked it over.
   George and Edna talked over the possibility of starting a new business.
   George and Edna talked over one possibility. (*or* . . . talked one possibility over)
3. The Jacksons have paid off all the debts that they once owed.
   The Jacksons have paid them off.
   The Jacksons have paid off their debts. (*or* . . . paid their debts off)
4. Do you believe we could build up enough business? (*or* . . . build enough business up)
   Do you believe we could build up enough business to succeed?
   Do you believe we could built it up?
5. We could take it over.
   We could take over that building. (*or* . . . take that building over)
   We could take over that empty building on Main Street.
6. We could work out agreements satisfactory to all of us.
   We could work them out.
   We could work out satisfactory agreements. (*or* . . . work satisfactory agreements out)
7. The clown took them off.
   The clown took off five shirts. (*or* . . . took five shirts off)
   The clown took off all the shirts that he had on.
8. The clown put it on.
   The clown put on a colorful hat. (*or* . . . put a colorful hat on)
   The clown put on a red, green, and yellow straw hat.
9. Robbers held up the bank at the corner of Sixth and Main.
   Robbers held up a bank. (*or* . . . held a bank up)
   Robbers held it up.
10. Edna picked them out.
    Edna picked out two tomatoes. (*or* . . . picked two tomatoes out)
    Edna picked out the two largest tomatoes she could find.

5. Trying Variations

1. Did George and Edna talk the matter over?
   George and Edna are talking the matter over.
   George and Edna may not talk the matter over.
2. The Jacksons are paying off all their debts.
   The Jacksons have paid off all their debts.
   The Jacksons cannot pay off all their debts.
3. The company may lay off thirty workers.
   The company has laid off thirty workers.
   Is the company laying off thirty workers?
4. Mr. Green sent for Mr. Jackson.
   Did Mr. Green send for Mr. Jackson?
   Why did Mr. Green send for Mr. Jackson?
5. The Jacksons may not take over an old building.
   The Jacksons have taken over an old building.
   Will the Jacksons take over an old building?
6. Has George met with the owner?
   George will meet with the owner.
   George met with the owner yesterday.

7. The owner was holding out for more rent.
   The owner may hold out for more rent.
   The owner has held out for more rent.
8. The Jacksons are sleeping on their decision.
   The Jacksons have slept on their decision.
   The Jacksons slept on their decision last night.

9. Will George tune up many small engines?
   George tuned up many small engines last month.
   George is tuning up many small engines.
10 The Jacksons will keep on trying.
   Will the Jacksons keep on trying?
   The Jacksons have kept on trying.

6. Making Up Original Sentences

Answers will vary.

CHAPTER 10

1. Reading

Oral work

2. Choosing the Right Word

1. agreed on
2. called off
3. back out of
4. part with
5. turn out
6. run out of
7. lived through
8. count on
9. shopped around
10. dealt with
11. checked up on
12. found out
13. making off with
14. turned down
15. singled out
16. lived up to
17. filled in
18. paid money down
19. went up
20. laid aside
21. cashed in
22. helped out
23. live off
24. cheer up
25. stick to
26. pay off
27. sell out
28. shut the business down
29. pitch in

3. Reading Aloud

Oral work

4. Using Passive Verbs

1. The amount of rent was agreed upon.
2. Other details were settled on.
3. Large profits cannot be counted on.
4. It cannot be called off now.
5. A large amount of money was made off with by one dealer.
6. One reliable company was singled out by the Jacksons.
7. Only the honest companies would be dealt with.
8. Many forms are filled in.

9. Some money is paid down on each purchase.
10. Some money had been laid aside.
11. Some bonds had been cashed in.
12. The business will never be sold out.
13. The business will never be shut down.
14. The building on Main Street has been taken over by the Jacksons.
15. Their business has been set up there.
16. Nine engines were tuned up by Mr. Jackson in one day.
17. The engines that they will sell have been picked out.
18. Many changes in their lives have been brought about by the new business.
19. A planned trip to Europe has been put off.
20. Much of their clothing has been worn out.

5. Using Two-Word Verbs with "Turn"

1. turned around
2. turned up
3. turned it down
4. turned his paper in
5. turn in
6. turn the matter over
7. turned the television on
8. turned it off
9. turn out
10. turned against
11. turned into
12. turn their small business into

6. Making Up Original Sentences

Answers will vary.

CHAPTER 11

1. Reading

Oral work

2. Choosing the Right Verb

1. disposed of
2. worked on
3. took in
4. paid out
5. did without
6. amount to
7. settle up
8. Putting up
9. hand out
10. take off
11. count out
12. sent away for
13. added up to
14. close out
15. mark up
16. buy out
17. bought out
18. sold off
19. marked down
20. dealt in
21. totaled up
22. sum up
23. lived on
24. carry on with
25. send out for

3. Using Two- and Three-Word Verbs

Answers will vary.

4. Using Two-Word Verbs with "Take"

1. took off
2. took off
3. take you on
4. take in

5. took up
6. take over
7. take Helen out

5. Using Two-Word Verbs with "Put"

1. put aside
2. put away
3. put their heads together
4. put off
5. putting up

6. put on
7. put down
8. put up with
9. put in

6. Using Two-Word Verbs with "Keep"

1. keep up
2. keep up with
3. kept on
4. kept on with (*or* kept at)
5. keep their expenses down
6. keep at
7. keep up (*or* keep up with, keep at; *or past tense*: kept up, kept up with, kept at)

7. Making Up Original Sentences

Answers will vary.

CHAPTER 12

1. Reading

Oral work

2. Substituting

1. cheered him on
2. show off
3. got behind
4. speeded up (*or* sped up)
5. caught up
6. slowed down

7. let up
8. hang on
9. came through
10. beat out
11. faced with
12. make up

13. push on
14. fight the other runners off
15. noses an opponent out
16. shut Dave out
17. laughed off
18. stand up for
19. turn against
20. back up
21. root for
22. stirring up
23. hold it against (Should you *hold* it *against* people . . .)
24. take on
25. speed up

3. Pronouncing

Oral work

4. Using Nouns Based on Two-Word Verbs

Answers will vary.

5. Forming Questions

1. Should we back up our team?
2. When did Tom beat out Dave in a race?
3. Who caught up with Dave in the last fifty meters?
4. Who carried off the victory?
5. Why did their friends cheer the runners on?
6. Do you usually try to come through with a victory?
7. Is everyone faced with difficulties in making good decisions?
8. Who must fight off troubles?
9. Is it true that all of us sometimes get behind?
10. Should we hold it against Dave if he loses again? (*or* Should we not hold . . .)
11. Can most people laugh off defeat?
12. What happens if a person lets up too soon?
13. How much distance did Tom make up?
14. Which horse nosed out Double Trouble and Old Harry?
15. When did the Giants pull far ahead?
16. Did the swimmers push on even when the waves began to get high?
17. Will students still root for the team?
18. Who showed off his speed?
19. Who did Helen usually side with?
20. Did both teams shut out their opponents?
21. Do drivers usually slow down on slick roads?
22. Who was speeding up and getting away?
23. What did my father always stand up for?
24. When did Edna stir up some new problems?
25. Who did Pedro and Fernando take on in a swimming contest?
26. Do most parents turn against a child who loses?

6. Making Up Original Sentences

Answers will vary.

CHAPTER 13

1. Reading

Oral work

2. Substituting

1. talk over
2. write up (*Also possible*: write out, write down)
3. came up
4. go about
5. go into
6. bring out
7. driving at
8. put down
9. looked up
10. write out
11. thumb through
12. pick out
13. stumble across

3. Substituting

1. sum up
2. dwell on
3. write down
4. became of
5. came out
6. make up
7. spun the story out
8. read up on
9. find out
10. subscribes to
11. dipped into
12. draw up
13. play up
14. turn out

4. Using Other Tenses

1. brought out, has brought out, may bring out
2. came out, has come out, should come out
3. came up, have come up, might come up
4. dwelled (*or* dwelt) on, has dwelled (*or* dwelt) on, did dwell on
5. found out, have found out, must find out
6. drew up, has drawn up, can draw up
7. went into, have gone into, do not go into
8. made up, has made up, may make up
9. put down, has put down, should put down
10. read up on, has read up on, will read up on
11. spun out, has spun out, could spin out
12. summed up, has summed up, will sum up
13. wrote down, has written down, should write down
14. wrote out, has written out, will write out
15. wrote up, have written up, must write up

5. Making Up Original Sentences

Answers will vary.

CHAPTER 14

1. Reading

Oral work

2. Answering Questions

(Answers may vary slightly.)

1. You speak about the person.
2. *Speak of* has the same meaning.
3. You speak for it.
4. You talk back to the person.
5. You talk down to the person.
6. *Talk up* has that meaning.
7. *Break in* has about the same meaning.
8. He or she breaks in on the conversation.
9. He or she breaks it off.
10. You may cry out.
11. You blurt it out.
12. The crowd may shout you down.
13. You are speaking out.
14. You touch on it.
15. You think of it.
16. You tell on her.
17. You talk on and on.
18. It goes on and on.

3. Using Verbs in Other Contexts

1. spoke about
2. thought of
3. shout him down
4. broke in on
5. talked on and on
6. speak out
7. blurt out
8. talk down to
9. talked that up
10. break off

4. Figuring Out Other Meanings

(Answers will vary but should have these meanings.)

1. He moved the car backward.
2. Burglars came in by breaking a window, lock, or something else.
3. He took the branch off (probably with his hands).
4. The recipe said that we should use two cups of flour.
5. They became less angry and stopped fighting.
6. The gun discharged (fired, was shot).
7. Trouble will end (go away, disappear).
8. She wanted to keep the noises out (make the room more quiet).
9. Do you agree with that belief?
10. The flood destroyed the bridge (carried the bridge away).
11. They usually solve their problems.

5. Making Up Original Sentences

Answers will vary.

CHAPTER 15

1. Reading

Oral work

2. Choosing the Right Verb

1. attends to
2. cheer up
3. heard about
4. grew up
5. allow for
6. occurred to
7. looking forward to
8. held up
9. look back on
10. passed up
11. put our heads together
12. put their toys away
13. put off
14. rang in
15. Look out
16. turned several possibilities over
17. tell them apart
18. Watch out
19. rule out
20. thought back
21. Think it over

3. Answering Questions

Answers will vary.

4. Choosing the Right Verb

1. overlook
2. overran
3. overtook
4. outsells
5. overdo
6. upset (*or* overturn)
7. inset
8. overcame
9. overturned (*or* upset)
10. uphold

5. Making Up Original Sentences

Answers will vary.

6. Making Up an Original Conversation

Answers will vary.

CUMULATIVE REVIEW

Review Exercises I

1. Using Objects of Separable Verbs

1. Let's check over our papers.
    Let's check our papers over.
    Let's check them over.
2. He crossed it out.
    He crossed a wrong answer out.
    He crossed out a wrong answer.
3. We found it out.
    We found the truth out.
    We found out the truth.
4. We should look up those articles.
    We should look those articles up.
    We should look them up.
5. I like to put these together.
    I like to put puzzles like this together.
    I like to put together puzzles like this.
6. We gave them away.
    We gave some food away.
    We gave away some food.
7. She had on some old shoes.
    She had some old shoes on.
    She had them on.
8. Jim didn't hang up his sweater.
    Jim didn't hang his sweater up.
    Jim didn't hang it up.
9. I tried to pick them up.
    I tried to pick the dishes up.
    I tried to pick up the dishes.
10. Have they used up all the soap?
    Have they used all the soap up?
    Have they used it up?

11. She left on her gloves.
    She left her gloves on.
    She left them on.
12. Please try on these shoes.
    Please try these shoes on.
    Please try them on.
13. Dave left out one problem.
    Dave left one problem out.
    Dave left it out.
14. Please shut off the water.
    Please shut the water off.
    Please shut it off.
15. Children quickly wear out their clothes.
    Children quickly wear their clothes out.
    Children quickly wear them out.
16. Tom asked her out.
    Tom asked Helen out.
    Tom asked out Helen.
17. The committee put it off.
    The committee put the celebration off.
    The committee put off the celebration.
18. Jane washed out some clothing.
    Jane washed some clothing out.
    Jane washed it out.
19. Edna wiped it off.
    Edna wiped the counter off.
    Edna wiped off the counter.
20. She left on the radio.
    She left the radio on.
    She left it on.

2. Using "-ing" Forms

(These are some possible sentences that could be written.)

1. She was looking for the cat.
2. I don't like getting up.
3. I am putting away my books.
4. That building is burning up.
5. The milk is boiling over.
6. He is sewing up a hole in his pocket.
7. They enjoy showing off.
8. She is handing in her examination paper.
9. They are looking at some paintings.
10. He was turning on all the lights.

11. She was dusting off the furniture.
12. The sky was clouding up.
13. He will be coming over soon.
14. She was waiting for a bus.
15. Mrs. Jackson was reading through several newspapers.
16. He was running out of time.
17. The baby was breaking the toys up.
18. Mr. Jackson was sweeping out the shop.
19. Jack was living on bread and water.
20. They are getting together to discuss their problems.

3. Using Past Participles

1. caught up with
2. given up
3. gone after
4. kept up with
5. made the examination up
6. put several potatoes in
7. read through
8. stood for
9. torn it up
10. come across
11. got (*or* gotten) up
12. hung up
13. let the cat in
14. run down
15. seen about
16. cut it up
17. done without
18. eaten up
19. put off
20. left the lights on
21. lain down
22. sat down
23. blown up
24. grown out of
25. set in
26. taken up
27. shut off
28. worn out
29. brought about
30. shown off

4. Using Past Tenses

1. caught up with
2. gave up
3. went after
4. kept up with
5. made the examination up
6. put several potatoes in
7. read through
8. stood for
9. tore it up
10. came across
11. got up
12. hung up
13. let the cat in
14. ran down
15. saw about
16. cut it up
17. did without
18. ate up
19. put off
20. left the lights on
21. lay down
22. sat down
23. blew up
24. grew out of
25. set in
26. took up
27. shut off
28. wore out
29. brought about
30. showed off

Review Exercises II

1. Making Up "Yes-No" Questions

1. Did George's father drop out of school?
2. Was George's father sorry that he once held up people?
3. Did he settle down later?
4. Did he and his wife usually pull together?
5. Should a person go back on a promise?
6. Do police sometimes line up suspected criminals?
7. Must a young person sometimes look for a job?
8. Do criminals sometimes get away?
9. Was the old man's death drawing near?
10. Has his wife always stood by him?

2. Making Up "Wh-" Questions

1. When did they head out toward Hillsdale?
2. Why did they turn around?
3. Where had Mrs. Jackson checked in?
4. When had the plane taken off?
5. Who dined out with her parents?
6. When did Edna dine out with her parents?
7. With whom did Edna dine out?
8. Why did a driver run off the road?
9. What did he run over?
10. Which tire blew out?

3. Using Intransitive Verbs

Answers will vary.

4. Varying Placement of Adverbs

(The adverb may be in any of the places marked by the caret ‸ .)

1. ‸ Helen ‸ looked ‸ for her mistake ‸ .
2. ‸ The old man ‸ looked ‸ back ‸ on his marriage ‸ .
3. ‸ Jim ‸ jacked up the car ‸ .
4. ‸ Edna ‸ put her coat on ‸ .
5. ‸ The driver ‸ plowed ‸ into a truck ‸ .
6. ‸ Tom ‸ backed ‸ out ‸ .
7. ‸ The noise ‸ went ‸ on ‸ .
8. ‸ George ‸ fixed the engine up ‸ .
9. ‸ The Jacksons ‸ had ‸ saved up money ‸ .
10. ‸ Prices ‸ were ‸ going up ‸ .

5. Using Negatives

1. We could not agree on the terms.
   We may not agree on the terms.
   We have not agreed on the terms.
   We are not agreeing on the terms.
2. The business does not pay off.
   The business did not pay off.
   The business may not pay off.
   The business must not pay off.
3. Mr. Jackson should not cheer up.
   Mr. Jackson may not cheer up.
   Mr. Jackson is not cheering up.
   Mr. Jackson did not cheer up.
4. Edna could not part with her old dishes.
   Edna would not part with her old dishes.
   Edna may not part with her old dishes.
   Edna has not parted with her old dishes.
5. Some people do not stick to their work.
   Some people did not stick to their work.
   Some people may not stick to their work.
   Some people are not sticking to their work.
6. Mr. Jackson does not count on help from his family.
   Mr. Jackson should not count on help from his family.
   Mr. Jackson could not count on help from his family.
   Mr. Jackson did not count on help from his family.
7. The Jacksons did not dine out often.
   The Jacksons may not dine out often.
   The Jacksons could not dine out often.
   The Jacksons are not dining out often.
8. The Jacksons would not sign up with a dishonest dealer.
   The Jacksons could not sign up with a dishonest dealer.
   The Jacksons must not sign up with a dishonest dealer.
   The Jacksons have not signed up with a dishonest dealer.
9. Helen does not pass out.
   Helen will not pass out.
   Helen has not passed out.
   Helen is not passing out.
10. She did not feel up to walking faster.
    She does not feel up to walking faster.
    She is not feeling up to walking faster.
    She has not felt up to walking faster.

6. Using Imperatives

(Here are three possible sentences for each command or request. Others may also be possible.)

1. Please cheer up. Do cheer up. Will you please cheer up.
2. Please pay off your debts. Pay your debts off. Do pay off your debts.
3. Please do the problem over. Will you do the problem over, please. Do over the problem.
4. Please don't back out of the agreement. Don't back out of the agreement, please. Do back out of the agreement.
5. Please do not turn down my offer. Do not turn my offer down. Do not turn down my offer, please.
6. Do turn around. Please turn around. Will you please turn around.
7. Do get into the car. Please get into the car. Get into the car, please.
8. Please ring for the nurse. Will you ring for the nurse. Do ring for the nurse.
9. Joe, please try out for the band. Do try out for the band, Joe. Will you please try out for the band, Joe.
10. Please take your shoes off. Take off your shoes. Do take your shoes off.

Review Exercises III

1. Placing Objects

1. Tom nosed out all the other runners in the race.
   Tom nosed them out.
   Tom nosed the other runners out.
   Tom nosed out the other runners.
2. George thought it over.
   George thought his problem over.
   George thought over his problem.
   George thought over what he could do to make the shop larger.
3. Edna handed them out.
   Edna handed out some gifts for the small children.
   Edna handed out several gifts.
   Edna handed several gifts out.
4. Edna summed up everybody's opinion.
   Edna summed everybody's opinion up.
   Edna summed up what everybody in the room was thinking.
   Edna summed it up.
5. The Jacksons may put up a larger building than they now have.
   The Jacksons may put up a larger building.
   The Jacksons may put a larger building up.
   The Jacksons may put it up.

2. Using the Passive Voice

1. Their prices were marked down.
2. Free pencils were handed out.
3. All the pencils must be counted up.
4. The first prize was carried off by a team from Pennsylvania.
5. Our team was shut out for ten minutes by the Pennsylvanians.
6. A few rebels were successfully fought off by soldiers.
7. Many original sentences are made up by students using this book.
8. A summary of the class discussion has been written up by Jim and Jane.
9. Some unpleasant remarks were blurted out by people in the audience.
10. The use of guns must be ruled out.

3. Using "-ing" Forms As Objects

Answers will vary.

4. Using Nouns Made from Two-Word Verbs

Answers will vary.

Verb Index

Page numbers refer to glossary entries or to other places where meanings are shown. Ellipses between the parts of a two-word verb show that a verb is separable; the object can be used in one place or the other. A blank line following a verb means that the verb is nonseparable; the object can be used only in that place.